Endeavor

⑥

New Readers Press®
ProLiteracy's publishing division

The following teachers participated in pilot testing of Endeavor:

Evelyn Surma, Adult Education Teacher
Anaheim Union High School District, Anaheim, CA

Maria Pagnotta, ABE-GED Professor
Seminole Community College, Sanford, FL

Rachel M. Slavkin, Adjunct Faculty
Seminole Community College, Sanford, FL

Lora Zangari, Professional Development Coordinator
Lancaster Lebanon IU13, Lancaster, PA

Endeavor 6
ISBN 978-1-56420-856-9

Printed in the United States of America
9 8 7 6

Proceeds from the sale of New Readers Press materials support professional development, training, and technical assistance programs of ProLiteracy that benefit local literacy programs in the U.S. and around the globe.

Contributing Author: Vista Resources, Inc.
Developmental Editors: Ellen Northcutt, Donna Townsend
Creative Director: Andrea Woodbury
Production Specialist: Maryellen Casey
Art and Design Supervisor: James P. Wallace
Illustrator: Kathleen Rietz, represented by Wilkinson Studios, Inc.

Contents

Smart Eating

Learning Objectives

In this lesson you will:

▓ Learn about childhood obesity.

▓ Learn to identify main idea and details.

▓ Master the key vocabulary used in the article.

▓ Write an explanation of how a parent can help an obese child lose weight.

Key Vocabulary

at risk *(adjective)* in danger

avoid *(verb)* to stay away from

encourage *(verb)* to persuade someone to do something *Khuyến Khích*

expert *(noun)* someone who knows a great deal about a particular thing *thành thạo*

joint *(noun)* the space where two body parts are joined together

lifestyle *(noun)* typical way of life for a person or group

obese *(adjective)* very overweight *béo phì*

portion *(noun)* a person's share of something, especially food *phần chia*

pressure *(noun)* the force produced by pressing on something *sức ép*

variety *(noun)* a lot of different things *≠ nhau nhiều*

Before You Read

As you begin to read this article, you know it will have something to do with being overweight. You can ask yourself this active reading question: What information will I find in this article? You can also ask yourself: What do I already know about this problem? These active reading strategies will help you concentrate and understand the article.

Make predictions while you read.

THINK ABOUT IT

From the picture and the title, I can tell that the article is about Shakira's problem with her weight. I know that overweight people often have health problems. Even though she's young, I guess that Shakira has some health problems.

1. Look at the title of the article. What is Shakira's problem?

   Shakira's problem is eat a lot of snack (chips, cookies, ...) non-healthy food

2. Look at the picture. What other problems do you think Shakira might have?

   Shakira being over weight because of eating too much fat food, snack, chips at night.

Use what you know.

THINK ABOUT IT

I'm thinking of my sister's son, who is heavy. He eats lots of junk food. His mother tried to get him to lose weight, but it didn't work. I'm worried about him.

1. Do you know a child who is very overweight? Why do you think that child is overweight?

   My mid sister being over weight. My sister was eat alot

2. How do some people you know try to help kids lose weight?

Goodbye Cookies, Hello Apples

Read the article to find out how to help overweight children lose weight. Highlight or underline three things people can do to help them.

When Shakira Johnson was eight years old, she had some serious health problems. She was 20 pounds overweight. Her blood pressure was high. She was tired much of the time, spending hours sitting on the couch, watching TV, or playing on the computer. At school, she had trouble with the other kids. "They won't play
5   with me," Shakira told her mother. "They tease me. They call me names."

Do you know a child who is overweight? Do Shakira's problems sound familiar? Many children in this country are heavy. But some children are more than just overweight. They're **obese.** They're so overweight that they're **at risk** for developing a **variety** of serious problems later in life. These may include heart
10   disease, diabetes , and problems with their **joints.** The extra weight puts **pressure** on their knees, making it both painful and difficult to walk.

Take a minute and think about some of the children you know or see on the bus or at the mall. You'll realize what many **experts** have been telling us: Over the last 20 years, childhood obesity has become a very real problem in the United States.

15   Shakira was lucky. Her mother realized that Shakira was in trouble. She knew that Shakira might be overweight all her life if she didn't make some changes while she was still young.

Her mother also knew that there was no better way to keep herself and her children healthy than by eating smart and staying fit as a family. So she started the
20   whole family on a healthier **lifestyle.** Along with her husband and son Michael, who was also overweight, the family made wiser food choices and became more active.

Says Michael, Shakira's brother, as he carries a basketball under his left arm and a bottle of water under his right, "My dad had better be careful on the court. I move a lot faster these days. And today I'm going to beat him!"

starbuck

obese : béo phì

blood pressure *(noun)*
the force with which blood moves around the body

diabetes *(noun)* tiểu đường
a disease in which the body cannot properly control the amount of sugar in the blood

knees : đầu gối.

1. What health problems can being obese cause?

Obese can make you have a blood pressure

2. What did Shakira's mother do to help her family get healthier?

Her mom let them eat healthier food

Continue reading the article to find one way to help an overweight child lose weight. Highlight or underline phrases that support that idea.

25   Happily for Shakira, many of her health problems went away when she lost weight. Over a year, she went from 75 pounds to 60 pounds. A slimmer child, she had more energy. Her blood pressure went down to normal. She was more social with the kids at school. She made new friends. She joined the track team.

There are many steps Shakira's mother could have taken to help Shakira. Let's
30   look at a few.

Table for Four, Please

It's always best to eat at home where you have control of what and how much is served. But rather than eat at home, many families today find it quicker and easier to eat at fast-food restaurants. While this is understandable, most fast-food
35   meals are full of calories . Eating those delicious fries and that great-tasting pizza on the go makes it easy to gain weight without even realizing it.

When it is impossible to **avoid** fast food, you can **encourage** children to order from the healthier choices on the menu, such as salads and low-fat meals. Said Shakira after losing weight, "I like burgers and fries. But I love being thin even more."

40   In addition to healthier choices, you can make children aware of **portion** sizes. Encourage them to eat smaller amounts of food, rather than large helpings. Show them that a piece of meat should be about the same size as the palm of your hand. Serve them an eight-ounce glass of milk, not a 12-ounce glass.

Finally, you can pack fresh fruit and vegetables or low fat cheese and crackers
45   before you leave the house. This will make it easier to get through the day without stopping at the first restaurant you see when the kids get hungry.

Skip the Sweet Stuff

When they're finished eating, most children ask for dessert. What kinds of dessert do they ask for? Chocolate-chip cookies? Vanilla ice cream? Of course
50   that's what they ask for. Cookies and ice cream taste good. But these desserts are high in calories and very unhealthy. They're filled with fat and sugar. You can help a child lose weight by keeping fattening desserts out of the kitchen. Keep a variety of healthy choices such as bananas, apples, and melons in your refrigerator instead.

For children who want an afternoon snack, be sure there are plenty of good
55   things for them to eat. Popcorn (without butter) or carrot sticks are much better choices than chips or candy.

calories *(noun)*
    units of energy in food

People often don't realize that some popular drinks can also be high in fat and calories and provide very little nutrition . Whether out or at home, cut down or do away with soft drinks. A single can of soda, for example, may have as many as 13 teaspoons of sugar. In addition to being bad for their teeth, all that sugar will cause kids to gain weight. Instead of soda, offer children low-fat milk, water, or diet soda.

nutrition (noun)
food that a body needs

3. What changes can parents make to help children eat healthier foods?

_____

_____

4. Why is soda so unhealthy?

_____

_____

Finish reading the article to learn more about keeping children healthy.

Jump In

What do these things have in common: a jump rope, a basketball, a bike? All three of them are fun things that can help children keep active. Moving around is one of the best ways for children to lose weight and keep it off.

Experts say that children should be active at least 60 minutes a day. That time can be broken up into shorter periods of time. At first it may be best to exercise in short, ten-minute periods.

There are many ways for kids to be active. Take them to the community swimming pool. Give them jump ropes and let them play outside with friends. Encourage them to ride bikes, play soccer, or dance.

The point is that exercise helps kids lose weight and strengthens muscles. Said Shakira's brother, "My dad started taking me to the basketball court in the playground. I learned some really good moves." Added his dad, "Michael has lost eight pounds so far. He's getting strong and quick. He's even sleeping better."

Another way to get kids to exercise is to give them chores that require them to be active. Have them walk the dog, wash the car, or mow the lawn. You can also model active choices by taking the stairs instead of the elevator or walking to the store instead of driving.

If you're worried about a child's weight, you can make a difference. Help him or her to make healthy choices and to keep active. And remember to make it fun so everyone will want to do it together.

5. Do you think it's possible for overweight children to lose weight and keep it off? Why or why not?

_____

_____

After You Read

Build a robust vocabulary.

Writing Sentences   Write a complete sentence to respond to each of the following questions or statements. Use the underlined word in your answer. Use the definitions on page 5 to help you.

1. How would you <u>encourage</u> someone to lose weight?

   _____

2. What health problems could an <u>obese</u> person have?

   _____

3. What is something you <u>avoid</u>?

   _____

4. What can you do to live a healthy <u>lifestyle</u>?

   _____

5. How large is a healthy <u>portion</u> of meat?

   _____

Sentence Completions   Complete each sentence using a word from the box.

at risk	avoid	encourage	experts	joints
lifestyle	obese	portion	pressure	variety

1. She took a warm bath because her _____ hurt.

2. Alan stopped the bleeding by putting _____ on the cut.

3. An obese person is _____ of getting a serious disease.

4. The _____ told Jim that he had to lose weight.

5. You can choose from a _____ of healthy meals at that new restaurant.

Word Building   A **prefix** is a group of letters added to the beginning of a word. When a prefix is added, a new word with a new meaning is formed. Look at the chart below. It shows some common prefixes and their meanings.

Prefix	Meaning
dis-	not
pre-	before
re-	again
un-	not

Read these words. What is the same about all of them? Each of the words has a prefix. Circle the prefix in each word.

disappear	unusual	prearrange	disagree	replay

Use the meaning of the prefix to help you figure out what the word means. Then use each one in a sentence. The first one is done for you.

1. disappear: _Billy seems to disappear whenever there's work to do around the house._

2. unusual: _____

3. prearrange: _____

4. disagree: _____

5. replay: _____

TIP: When you read, you may find a long word that you do not recognize. Does the word begin with a prefix? Look closely to see if the word has a prefix you know. What does the prefix mean?

Writing Activity Write a short paragraph that correctly uses key vocabulary words to tell what an obese child can do to try to lose weight. Use at least four of the words from the list on page 5. Reread the definitions, if necessary.

_____

_____

_____

_____

Think about your reading.

Check your comprehension.   Answer each question. If you don't know the answer, reread the lines in parentheses.

1. What is one health problem an obese person may have? (lines 9–11)

_____

2. What is one thing a family can do to help an overweight child lose weight? (lines 37–46)

_____

3. How much exercise should a child get per day? (line 67)

_____

4. Name an example of a good outdoor exercise for an overweight child. (lines 70–72)

_____

Use reading skills: Identify main idea and details.

The **main idea** is the most important point an author makes about a subject. The ideas that tell about the main idea are called **details.** Sometimes, you will have to figure out the main idea by putting the details together.

Identify main idea and details. The main idea of the second paragraph of the article is that obese kids are in danger of getting serious illnesses later in life. The supporting details are found in the paragraph. Read the paragraph.

> Do you know a child who is overweight? Do Shakira's problems sound familiar? Many children in this country are heavy. But some children are more than just overweight. They're obese. They're so overweight that they're at risk of developing a variety of serious problems later in life. These may include heart disease, diabetes, and problems with their joints. The extra weight puts pressure on their knees, making it both painful and difficult to walk.

Main idea: Obese kids are in danger of getting serious illnesses later in life.

1. What is one illness an obese person may get later in life?

    Detail: _____

2. What is another illness an obese person may get?

    Detail: _____

3. How does being overweight affect the knees? What is it difficult to do then?

    Detail: _____

Use a graphic organizer.

In the chart below, there is a sentence that tells the main idea and a sentence that gives a supporting detail. Fill in the missing information.

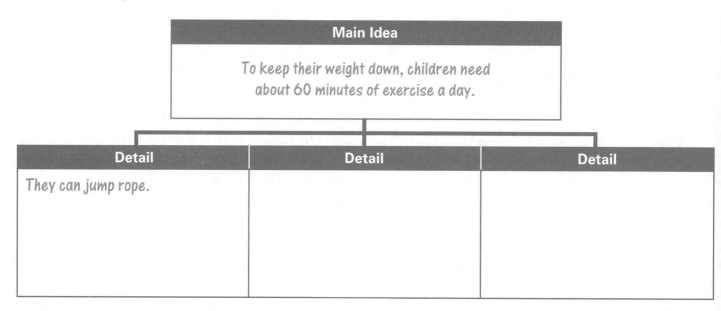

Write About It

Write an explanation.

A friend writes to you about her son Alex. She says that her son is overweight and needs to slim down for health and social reasons. Write a letter to your friend explaining what she can do to help her son.

Prewriting On your own or with a partner, write down suggestions that will help Alex lose weight. Think of suggestions that you have read about or know from experience. Fill in the graphic organizer with your ideas, writing your main idea and five details to support it.

Main Idea
How can a parent help a heavy child lose weight?

Detail	Detail	Detail

Detail	Detail

Thinking Beyond Reading   Think about these questions and discuss them with a partner. Add ideas to the graphic organizer as you talk.

- What foods may cause a child to gain weight?

- What are some examples of healthy desserts?

- How much exercise should a child get each day?

- What are some ways a child can exercise?

- Do you think these ideas can change someone's life? Why or why not?

Write a draft.   Write a first draft paragraph to answer your friend's letter. Your explanation should include a main idea and supporting details. You might begin with this sentence: "To help your son lose weight, you can change his eating and exercise habits." Use the details you listed on your chart to complete your explanation. Add as many details as you can.

_____

_____

_____

_____

_____

_____

_____

_____

_____

_____

_____

_____

_____

_____

_____

Revise and create a final draft.   Write your final draft on a separate piece of paper. As you revise, check your draft for these specific points:

- Did you write a topic sentence that sums up the main point of the paragraph?

- Did you include details that support the main idea?

- Did you check spelling and grammar to make sure your writing is clear and correct?

Growing Your Job Possibilities

Learning Objectives

In this lesson you will:

◼ Read a story about one man's job at a plant nursery.

◼ Learn to recognize cause and effect.

◼ Master the key vocabulary used in the story.

◼ Write a description of how to grow healthy roses.

Key Vocabulary

artificial *(adjective)* made by humans; not natural

conferred *(verb)* talked together; discussed

dreading *(verb)* fearing

forged *(verb)* formed through hard work

fragrant *(adjective)* having a sweet or pleasant smell

luscious *(adjective)* appealing to the senses

maintenance *(noun)* upkeep

mature *(adjective)* fully grown

regional *(adjective)* related to a specific area

trowel *(noun)* a small scoop-shaped tool used for gardening

Before You Read

As you begin to read a story about a man's love of roses, think about what you know about growing plants. Then, as you continue to read, use the active reading strategy of visualizing, or picturing in your mind the events and descriptions in the story. The author will help you visualize by using words and phrases that appeal to your senses of sight, sound, smell, taste, and touch.

Use what you know.

THINK ABOUT IT

1. Have you ever seen a rose? What does it look like? What do roses smell like?

   _____

   _____

   _____

My brother and I used to grow tomato plants. We watered them and pulled out the weeds. It was a lot of work, especially in the hot summer, but we loved to eat the tomatoes we grew.

2. Do you know people who do gardening? What kinds of things do they do in their gardens?

   _____

   _____

   _____

Visualize as you read.

THINK ABOUT IT

Read the first four paragraphs.
1. What things tell you Mr. Rodriquez is ready to work?

   _____

   _____

   _____

   _____

I picture a young boy. His father comes into the room carrying tools and looking like he's ready to start using them.

2. What is Gil doing when his father says it's time to plant?

   _____

   _____

   _____

   _____

For a Love of Roses

Read the story to find out about Gil's relationship with his father. Highlight phrases that show how their interest in gardening brought the two closer.

"It's because of Papa. And his love of roses." That is what Gilberto Rodriquez says started him on the path to his later position as owner and president of Cloverdale Nursery. It was Gil's childhood experiences in the family backyard that led to his lifelong passion for gardening.

5   It began on a bright spring day, when Gil was just eight years old. "Come on," Mr. Rodriquez said. He was carrying a **trowel** and spade on his way to the yard.

"Where to?" asked Gil, as he lay on the living room sofa. "I'm watching cartoons."

"Out. It's time to plant the rose bushes," Mr. Rodriquez responded, putting on a pair of work gloves.

10   "Why?"

"Because it's spring." And he scooted his son out to their backyard.

"Roses are the most beautiful flowers there are," Papa began, shaking a rose bush from a pot. "If tended properly, they will give you endless joy. Remember that."

Papa pointed to the five rose bushes he had purchased earlier that morning.

15   "Find a spot that gets lots of sun," Papa advised.

"What about here?" Gil suggested, pointing to a shady spot.

"No good. Roses need at least six hours of sun a day. Shade is no good. Come on. Grab a shovel. It's time to dig."

1. How did gardening with his father affect Gil's life?

_____

_____

2. What kind of relationship do Gil and his dad seem to have?

_____

_____

Continue reading the story to find out how a love of roses helped Gil's relationship with his dad. Highlight or mark sentences that help you visualize what Gil and his father did with the rose bushes.

Gil and Papa worked all morning—spacing and digging the holes, adding lime,
20 planting the bushes, and filling the holes with rich soil. By midday Gil was hot and sweaty, but he was enjoying himself anyway. Gil had fun sharing the tools, watering the plants, even spraying Papa with a water hose. And best of all, three months later, in the height of summer, Gil and his dad filled their house with the **fragrant** roses that had bloomed in the yard—tall, elegant red roses, white English
25 roses, and pink, long-stemmed tea roses.

"Nothing better than this," Papa said proudly, glancing around the flower-filled living room.

As years went by, caring for the rose bushes **forged** a special bond between Gil and Papa. From spring through early fall, Gil and his father talked about the roses'
30 **maintenance** and progress. Together, the two checked on the soil. They **conferred** about drainage. They pruned and they watered. Come summer, they snipped the **mature** flowers, patting each other on the back as they worked together to put the **luscious** flowers in vases around the house.

When Gil turned 16, his thoughts turned to girls. Gil was starting to date, and
35 he needed money to take out a pretty neighbor named Maria. So, at his father's suggestion, Gil got a job at a local nursery, caring for the hundreds of plants, shrubs, and flowers there. By this time, Gil loved gardening. So, because he was surrounded by plants at work, he looked forward to his job every day.

Some years later, after Gil graduated from college, he was offered a job as
40 manager of Cloverdale Nursery. The owners were looking for someone with special traits: an individual with a good business sense, responsible, excellent with customers, and with a "green thumb." Gil was perfect for the job.

"I love it," he told his father over the phone. Gil didn't have time to visit his parents much any more, but he kept up with his family through e-mail and phone calls.
45 As time went on, Gil's financial needs grew. He was now 31, married, with two kids, and a mortgage . So, when the owners of the company offered him a position as **regional** manager, Gil accepted. The new job would give him much more pay, something he needed as expenses at home increased.

mortgage (noun)
a loan to buy property

3. What things did Gil and his dad do together with the roses?

_____

_____

4. How are Gil and his father alike?

_____

_____

Finish reading the story. As you read, continue to visualize what's going on.

But Gil's new job also brought dissatisfaction. Gil no longer spent his days
outdoors in the sun. He rarely met with customers, which he once loved. He no
longer had time to offer advice about where to plant the rose bushes or what garden
equipment to buy. No, now Gil worked indoors, at a computer, under **artificial**
light. His days were spent analyzing spreadsheets and conducting meetings.
Sometimes he got out of the office, but that was only to get in his car and drive to
corporate headquarters . There he and other managers discussed profit margins .
"The pay is great, Papa," he told his father over the phone one day. "But the
job's not what I love."
"What do you love, son?" asked his dad.
"Roses," was Gil's reply.
Years later, the Cloverdale Nursery owners decided to sell their business, and
Gil couldn't refuse the opportunity. At age 45, he became owner and president of
the company, and, for the next 20 years, he managed the business. By that time,
the business had grown and so had Gil's son and daughter.
One day, Gil received a phone call he had been **dreading.** His ailing father
had passed away during the night. Gil took the loss hard. He thought about his
life. He had a beautiful house and a family he loved. But he wasn't doing what he
wanted. So he discussed the situation with his wife Maria, and they agreed.
Gil sold the company to his children and retired. From that day on, he spent
most of his days in his backyard tending to the rose bushes. He filled his house
with vases of tall, elegant red roses, white English roses, and pink, long-stemmed
tea roses.
But Gil's happiest days were when he was telling his eight-year-old
granddaughter to turn off the TV and pick up a trowel. "Look for a spot that gets
plenty of sun," he said just the other day. "If tended properly," Gil said, as he
handed the girl a plant, "roses will give you endless joy."

50
55
60
65
70
75

spreadsheets *(noun)*
    accounting charts

corporate headquarters
    (noun)
    main place of business
    for a company

profit margins *(noun)*
    the amount of money
    made after expenses
    are paid

5. What caused Gil to retire?

_____

_____

6. What do you think Gil's granddaughter will do for a hobby when she grows
   up? Why?

_____

_____

After You Read

Build a robust vocabulary.

Writing Sentences   Write a complete sentence to respond to each of the following questions or statements. Use the underlined word in your answer. Use the definitions on page 15 to help you.

1.   What is something <u>fragrant</u> you've smelled lately?

_____

2.   What regular <u>maintenance</u> does a car need?

_____

3.   What is one responsibility of a <u>regional</u> manager for a nursery chain?

_____

4.   What kinds of events are you or a friend <u>dreading</u>?

_____

5.   Describe a <u>mature</u> rose bush.

_____

Sentence Completions   Complete each sentence using a word from the box.

artificial	conferred	dreading	forged	fragrant
luscious	maintenance	mature	regional	trowel

1.   Benny disliked working in an office with _____ light.

2.   Rodrigo stopped to admire the _____ flowers.

3.   We _____ about the best place to have the party.

4.   Let's use the _____ to dig up the soil.

5.   We _____ a bond with our neighbors and spent many happy times with them.

Word Building   A **suffix** is a group of letters added to the end of a word. When a suffix is added, a new word with a new meaning is formed. The suffix -*ment* means the "act or result of." *Achievement* is the act of achieving. *Contentment* is the result of feeling content.

Draw a circle around the suffix in each word. Then write a sentence using the word.

1. amazement: _____

2. entertainment: _____

3. amusement: _____

4. encouragement: _____

5. disappointment: _____

TIP: When you come across a word you do not know, see if the word has a suffix, or ending, you recognize such as -*ment* in *achievement*. If you know what the suffix means, you may be able to figure out the meaning of the word.

Writing Activity   Write a short paragraph that correctly uses key vocabulary words to tell about something good that happened at work. Write what you saw, heard, smelled, tasted, or touched. Use at least four of the words from the list on page 15. Reread the definitions, if necessary.

_____

_____

_____

_____

Think about your reading.

Check your comprehension.   Answer each question. If you don't know the answer, reread the lines in parentheses.

1. What do rose bushes need to grow? (line 17)

_____

2. What happened when Gil got out of college? (lines 39–40)

_____

3. Why did Gil accept the job of regional manager at Cloverdale Nursery? (lines 45–48)

_____

4. What was one thing Gil liked about his job as regional manager at the nursery? (line 56)

_____

5. Why did Gil retire? (lines 65–67)

_____

Use reading skills: Identify cause and effect.

Many events in our lives have causes and effects. A **cause** brings about other events in a story. An **effect** is the result of a cause. For example, rain starts to fall. That's a cause. People open their umbrellas. That's an effect.

In addition to an event, a cause can be an action, a feeling, or a situation. In the story 16-year-old Gil wanted to find a job. The cause was Gil wanting to date a girl. The effect was that Gil got a job to pay for his dates.

Identify cause and effect.   In the following paragraph, you learn the many causes of Gil's unhappiness at work.

> But Gil's new job also brought dissatisfaction. Gil no longer spent his days outdoors in the sun. He rarely met with customers, which he once loved. He no longer had time to offer advice about where to plant the rose bushes or what garden equipment to buy. No, now Gil worked indoors, at a computer, under artificial light. His days were spent analyzing spreadsheets and conducting meetings.

List the causes of Gil's unhappiness at work.

1. _____

2. _____

3. _____

4. _____

5. _____

6. _____

Use a graphic organizer.

Sometimes one effect has several causes. You can use a graphic organizer to list an effect and its causes. Use the information in the story to help you fill in the causes for the effect given in the graphic organizer below.

Causes	Effect
1.	The owners of Cloverdale Nursery hired Gil as manager.
2.	
3.	
4.	

Write About It

Write a description.

You are the manager of a rose nursery. A customer writes to you for help. The rose bushes she bought at your nursery have failed. Read her letter below. Then write a response describing what she should do in the future to get healthy plants.

Dear Sir:

Last fall, I bought five rose bushes at your store. I planted them immediately. I put them in the shade. I admit that I forgot to water them. Two plants died, and three never grew or blossomed. Why did the plants die? Why didn't the others grow?

Please tell me what I did wrong. I love roses and want a garden full of them. What should I do?

Thank you.

——Mrs. Ramirez

Prewriting On your own or with a partner, fill in the graphic organizer for the two effects given below. First, write three mistakes the customer made that caused the rose bushes to fail. Then list three actions that will produce healthy rose bushes.

Causes	Effects
1.	Plants died or wouldn't grow.
2.	
3.	
4.	Rose bushes will grow well.
5.	
6.	

Thinking Beyond Reading   Think about these questions and discuss them with a partner. Add ideas to the graphic organizer as you talk.

- What kind of light do roses need?

- What kind of soil do roses need?

- In what season should rose bushes be planted?

- Why is it important to water rose bushes?

- What can be added to the soil to help the plants grow?

Write a draft.   Write a first draft of your description. Your paragraph might begin with this topic sentence: "There are several things that may have caused your plants to fail." Explain what those were. Use the details you listed in your graphic organizer to complete your paragraph. Continue with, "Next year, do the following things to grow healthy rose bushes."

_____

_____

_____

_____

_____

_____

_____

_____

_____

_____

_____

_____

_____

_____

Revise and create a final draft.   Write your final draft on a separate piece of paper. As you revise, check your draft for these specific points:

- Did you describe what caused the bushes to die or fail to grow?

- Did you tell what would cause rose bushes to grow well?

- Did you check spelling and grammar to make sure your writing is clear and correct?

A New Kind of Family

Learning Objectives

In this lesson you will:

▨ Learn about grandfamilies.

▨ Learn to classify ideas into categories.

▨ Master the key vocabulary used in the article.

▨ Write an e-mail to a friend.

Key Vocabulary

assistance *(noun)* aid or help

financial *(adjective)* relating to money

grateful *(adjective)* appreciative

issues *(noun)* concerns

neglect *(verb)* to fail to take care of

pampers *(verb)* gives someone a lot of attention

role *(noun)* the job someone has in a particular situation

sacrifice *(noun)* the act of giving something up

thrive *(verb)* to become successful, to grow

violence *(noun)* behavior that hurts other people physically

Before You Read

The article you are about to read is about grandparents and grandchildren. Here are some active reading strategies you can use to get the most out of the article. To get started, ask yourself what experience you've had with grandparents. As you read, continue to ask and answer questions to make sure you understand what you're reading.

Use what you know.

1. What experiences have you or a family member had with a grandparent?

   _____

   _____

   _____

2. Which experience with a grandparent stands out most in your mind?

   _____

   _____

   _____

3. Do you know other people who have a grandparent? What special experience do you know they have shared with that relative?

   _____

   _____

   _____

Ask yourself questions.

1. Why would a grandparent have to raise a child?

   _____

   _____

   _____

2. What would that relationship be like?

   _____

   _____

   _____

THINK ABOUT IT

I remember when my grandma made Thanksgiving dinner for the whole family. She did a great job, but she was so tired from all the work that everyone pitched in to help. I wonder if the article will talk about something like that.

THINK ABOUT IT

Why can't parents raise their own kids? Are they in the military? Are they sick? I'll read on to see why.

"Grandma, I'm Home!"

Read the article to find out what a grandfamily is. Use sticky notes to keep track of questions that come up as you read.

Do you have a favorite relative who makes you feel especially loved? Perhaps that relative is a grandmother or grandfather. Many of us feel wonderful when we spend time with a grandparent. Let's face it, we look forward to visiting Grandpa in his home. We feel important when Grandma

5 has cooked us a special dish. Said 12-year-old Lewis, who visits his grandma every Sunday, "She makes chicken for me and my brother. She wraps cookies and puts them in our pockets. I love Grandma."

Lewis' relationship with his grandmother is special because she **pampers** the boys and wants to spend as much time with them as possible. "I love my

10 mother, too," Lewis says. "But Mom makes me throw out the garbage. She gets after me about homework. She's not like Grandma. Grandma lets me be."

In the last 25 years, more grandparents are taking charge of everyday responsibilities for their grandkids in the same way parents do. More children are living with their grandparents than ever before. Grandparents these days

15 are changing diapers. They're making sure homework gets done. They're cooking all the meals. Grandparents are acting like parents because some parents can no longer do that job.

Problems Mean Change

Latoya lived with her mother and father in a downtown apartment in the city.

20 Everything was fine until Latoya turned eight. Around that time, Latoya's father moved out and her mother started using drugs. Latoya's mother was different and so was life at home. Sometimes her mom stayed out late or didn't come home at all. Sometimes there was no food in the house. Sometimes there was

social workers *(noun)*
   people who are trained to help people with social problems

legal guardian *(noun)*
   a person with the legal responsibility to care for another

25 no one to walk Latoya to school and she'd get there late. Her teachers noticed that something wasn't right. In time, social workers took Latoya away from her mother and placed her with her grandmother. Latoya's grandmother became her legal guardian . She cared for Latoya like a parent. They became a grandfamily.

Once Latoya moved in with her grandmother, she rarely heard from her mother. "I miss her," the girl said. "But she was never around. I needed her. My 30 grandmother is my mom now. It feels pretty good." Said Latoya's grandmother, "I wasn't going to let Latoya end up anywhere else. We're family and we're doing just fine."

Knock, Knock

Drug problems aren't the only reasons grandparents end up raising their 35 grandchildren. "One day a cop showed up at my door," said Ross, a 60-year-old man living in Chicago. "I could tell he had bad news. He told me that my son and daughter-in-law had been killed in a car accident." Ross said he knew at once that he and his wife would raise their grandchildren. "I lost my son," he said. "There was no way I was going to lose his kids, too."

40 Sometimes a parent wants to raise his or her own children, but for a variety of reasons, that's not possible. Sometimes illness gets in the way. Serious diseases such as cancer can make it difficult to care for children. In those cases, children may live with a grandparent or the grandparent may visit every day to cook and clean when mom or dad is just too sick.

45 More often than not, grandparents are happy to help out. "When my daughter was going through chemotherapy , she needed me, but her kids needed me, too. So I did what I could," said Pedro and Marta's grandmother. "Sure, I was tired, but I couldn't **neglect** them," she continued. "I bought their clothes. I helped with homework. I took them to the park. I was doing what 50 their mother couldn't."

Of course there are other reasons why grandparents get custody of their grandchildren. Sometimes the parents are unemployed and need to spend time looking for work. Other times, there is **violence** in the home and it's unsafe for the children to stay there. At still other times, a parent is in jail and Grandma 55 and Grandpa must raise the kids until Mom or Dad gets out.

chemotherapy *(noun)*
   the use of chemicals to treat cancer

custody *(noun)*
   the legal right to take care of a child

1. What are the feelings some grandparents might have about raising a grandchild after already raising their own kids?

   _____

   _____

2. How do you think some children feel about being raised by a grandparent, rather than a parent? Explain.

   _____

   _____

Finish reading the article. Find out which of your questions were answered.

What About Me?

How do these grandparents feel about their new **role?** After all, they've already raised their kids and thought that they would now have time for themselves. Most of them say they are happy. They say being with their
60 grandchildren keeps them young and active. They say that raising their grandchildren gives them a greater purpose for living.

But others are not as happy. Often they are so busy with the grandchildren that they have little time to take care of themselves. They may be short on money or feel that they're giving up their freedom. Yet they do it anyway.
65 "I made a **sacrifice,** but it had to be done," said Angela, "I didn't want a stranger raising the grandkids. I love them too much to let that happen."

As for the children themselves, many are **grateful** that a grandparent is looking after them. But their lives are not problem-free. "At school," said one young girl, "the other kids tease me because I don't live with my mom and dad."

70 ## Help Is Already Here

Fortunately there are organizations that assist with all sorts of grandfamily **issues.** Many states, for example, provide **financial** aid to help grandparents pay the bills.

There are other kinds of **assistance,** too. Grandparents in Florida can call a
75 special telephone helpline for advice on everything from health care to homework.

The city of Boston built Grandfamilies House especially for these special families. Grandfamilies House has 26 apartments with ramps outside for anyone who might have trouble with stairs. There's a bright colorful room where young children can play and another room where older kids and
80 grandparents can take computer classes together. It's a place where everyone in the grandfamily can **thrive.**

Grandparents and the organizations that help them have one thing in common. They want to do the best they can to raise happy, healthy children who will grow into successful adults.

ramps *(noun)*
slopes that connect two places that are at different levels

3. What is one question you asked earlier that was answered in this article? Write the question and the answer.

_____

_____

4. What is one question you asked earlier that was not answered in the article? Where might you find the answer?

_____

_____

After You Read

Build a robust vocabulary.

Writing Sentences   Write a complete sentence to respond to each of the following questions or statements. Use the underlined word in your answer. Use the definitions on page 25 to help you.

1.   What is one <u>financial</u> concern of yours?

_____

2.   Tell about a <u>sacrifice</u> you've made.

_____

3.   What are some <u>issues</u> in today's news?

_____

4.   Describe a time when you felt <u>grateful</u>.

_____

5.   Tell one way a teacher can help his or her students <u>thrive</u>.

_____

Sentence Completions   Complete each sentence using a word from the box.

assistance	financial	grateful	issues	neglect
pampers	role	sacrifice	thrive	violence

1.   She _____ her puppy with baths and treats.

2.   Tony took on the _____ of big brother after his sister was born.

3.   If you _____ your plants, they will die.

4.   Melinda needed _____ when she broke her leg.

5.   Everyone is concerned about _____ in the Middle East.

Word Building   Look at the following words. What is the same about them?

downhill	dishwasher	pillowcase	chalkboard

Each word is made up of two smaller words. They are **compound words.**

Draw a line between the two parts of each word. Compare answers with a partner. Discuss what each word means. Use the meaning of each part of the word to help you define the word.

Read the following compound words. What is the same in each compound word?

| daylight | daytime | daydream | daybreak |

Use each compound word in a sentence. The first one is done for you.

1. daylight: _Daylight flooded the room when I opened the window._

2. daytime: _____

3. daydream: _____

4. daybreak: _____

TIP: When you read, you may find a long word that you don't recognize. Does the word have two smaller words combined to make one word? Look closely to see if the word is a compound word.

Writing Activity   Write a short paragraph that correctly uses key vocabulary words to tell about Grandfamilies House or other programs available to grandfamilies. Use at least four of the words from the list on page 25. Reread the definitions, if necessary.

_____

_____

_____

_____

Think about your reading.

Check your comprehension.   Answer each question. If you don't know the answer, reread the lines in parentheses.

1. What has been happening to some families in the last 25 years? (lines 12–17)

_____

2. What is one reason grandparents raise their grandchildren? (lines 34–42)

_____

3. What other problems may cause a grandparent to raise grandkids? (lines 51–55)

_____

4. What kind of assistance can grandparents who are raising grandchildren get? (lines 72–75)

_____

Use reading skills: Classify information.

When you **classify,** you sort information into groups. You think how or why ideas or things go together. Classifying helps you understand and remember what you read. For example, you could classify reasons why grandparents raise their grandchildren by whether the reasons are permanent or temporary.

Classify information.   Reread this part of the article. It gives examples of reasons why grandparents sometimes raise their grandchildren.

> Sometimes the parents are unemployed and need to spend time looking for work. Other times, there is violence in the home and it's unsafe for the children to stay there. At still other times, a parent is in jail and Grandma and Grandpa must raise the kids until Mom or Dad gets out.

1.   What are two reasons why grandparents sometimes raise their grandchildren?

_____

2.   What do all the ideas in the paragraph have in common?

_____

Use a graphic organizer.

You can use a graphic organizer like the one below to help you classify information. Fill in the chart with temporary and long-term reasons why grandparents have to take care of their grandchildren. Use your own ideas and what you learned in the article.

Temporary Reasons	Long-Term Reasons
A parent is sick.	Both parents are dead.

Write About It

Write an e-mail.

Imagine you are a grandparent and your 4-year-old grandchild will be coming to live with you. The child's parent is your son who is divorced and uses drugs. Write an e-mail to a friend explaining how you feel about your grandchild living with you.

Prewriting   On your own or with a partner, write down ideas. Tell whether you would or wouldn't want your grandchild living with you and why. Think about how it would change your life. Fill in the graphic organizer with reasons that support your decision.

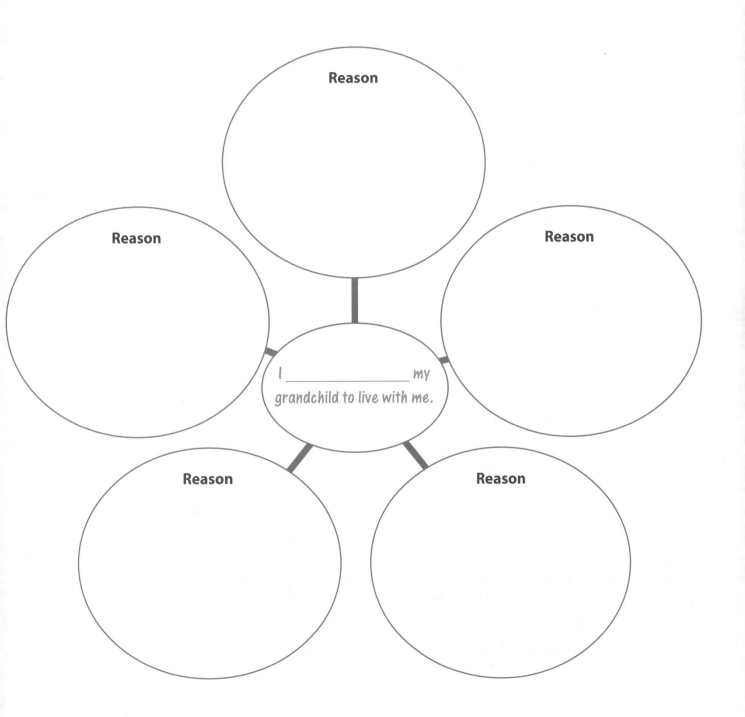

Thinking Beyond Reading   Think about these questions and discuss them with a partner. Add ideas to the graphic organizer as you talk.

- What is the family problem?

- How is the child doing?

- Why do you think you should or should not take care of your grandchild?

Write a draft.   Write a first draft of your e-mail. You might begin with this topic sentence: "I want my grandson to live with me because I am worried about him." Use the details you listed in your graphic organizer to complete your paragraph.

_____

_____

_____

_____

_____

_____

_____

_____

_____

_____

_____

_____

_____

_____

_____

Revise and create a final draft.   Write your final draft on a separate piece of paper. As you revise, check your draft for these specific points:

- Did you write a topic sentence that gives the main point of the e-mail?

- Did you check spelling and grammar to make sure your writing is clear and correct?

Friends and Neighbors

Learning Objectives

In this lesson you will:

▨ Read a story about a young man and a small store in a crisis.

▨ Learn to identify cause and effect.

▨ Master the key vocabulary used in the story.

▨ Write a summary paragraph that tells what happens in the story.

Key Vocabulary

abandoned *(verb)* gave up

frantically *(adverb)* in a very fast and excited way

generations *(noun)* different age levels in families: children, parents, grandparents; groups of people born at about the same time

horizontally *(adverb)* across; parallel to the ground

meticulously *(adverb)* in a very careful way

permeated *(verb)* spread throughout

preceding *(verb)* going before

receded *(verb)* moved back

tantrum *(noun)* a childish fit of bad temper

torrent *(noun)* an outpouring; a flood

Before You Read

When you read this story, use the strategies of visualizing the places and events the author tells you about and predicting what will happen. You might wonder what part a storm plays in the story. Make a prediction and think of it as you read to find out if you were right.

Make predictions about the story.

THINK ABOUT IT

1. What part do you think a storm will play in the story?

   _____

   _____

   _____

   _____

I wonder if something is going to change, that something will shake things up. I will have to read to find out if I'm right.

2. What do you think Jesse will be like? What clue do these sentences in the first paragraph give you about him: "Jesse sighed. It was always the same."

   _____

   _____

   _____

   _____

   _____

Visualize.

THINK ABOUT IT

1. What picture of the neighborhood do you get in your mind with cups and cigarette butts on the sidewalk and the metal cover over the storefront?

   _____

   _____

   _____

   _____

   _____

I can picture a whole street of little stores and all the people and other things you see there.

After the Storm

Jesse is feeling trapped. Highlight or mark sentences that tell what is bothering Jesse.

Eight in the evening, and Jesse was once again shutting up the shop while his father swept the crumpled cups and cigarette butts from the sidewalk. Jesse sighed. It was always the same. Every morning and evening, his father **meticulously** swept the front walk. Then, every evening, he rolled down the metal cover over the
5 storefront, carefully padlocked the cover, and headed home for dinner.

Sometimes Jesse thought if he had to work one more day in the little bodega, he would go stark, raving mad. The little store had been in the family for three **generations,** beginning with Grandpop Santiago. Grandpop had run it with Jesse's father Rene until Grandpop died. Now, Jesse was helping his father run the store.
10 Sometimes, Jesse could see nothing but despair ahead, a future of endless days of selling bananas, dime candy, and cigarettes to people he'd known his whole life.

"Evening," nodded Mrs. Aguirro as she tottered by, her cane **preceding** her with a clunk on every step. "How's that sister of yours?"

"She's good," Jesse nodded back. "Her baby just turned one."

15 "Well, isn't that something." Mrs. Aguirro beamed, as if a baby growing older were a remarkable achievement. "Isn't that something."

Jesse sighed, slipped on his jacket, and walked silently home with his dad. "What's wrong?" his dad asked.

Jesse shrugged. "You know. I just—" The words came out in a **torrent.**
20 "My future—my whole life—doing this? What am I doing? Nothing!"

Jesse's father was silent. "It's a family thing. It's a community thing. A tradition. We're part of this community. I guess I always hoped you'd want to be part of that, like Grandpop and me."

"I don't know," Jesse said, shaking his head. "I want to get out. I want to see
25 stuff. I don't want to spend my whole life in this place. Sorry, but that's how I feel."

bodega *(noun)*
a small grocery store, often in a Hispanic neighborhood

After his outburst, Jesse felt a little embarrassed, like a little kid who had a **tantrum** about not getting enough ice cream. His dad didn't bring up the subject again. Neither did Jesse.

1. How do you think Jesse's father felt after Jesse's outburst?

_____

_____

Read on to see what happens to Jesse. In the next section, underline the sentences that tell how he is feeling about his life and his job.

Warnings about a coming storm began during the evening news. "You can expect
30   several inches of rain," the forecaster said with a slight chuckle, as if the storm were a joke he'd invented. Jesse, still worrying about his life, noted the chatter without interest. It was spring. Of course it rained here. Gray days were as common as dirt.

Once the rain began, though, it didn't end. It rained for days. In alarm, the residents saw that the river was rising. The police and firefighters pulled on their
35   slickers and headed for the river with trucks full of sandbags. Volunteers joined them, standing with water dripping down their faces as the cold rain whipped **horizontally** past their rainproof hoods. They handed over the sandbags, person to person, piling them to keep the water from jumping the riverbank. Jesse's dad had headed into the store early, made an urn of coffee, and was passing it out with donuts to the volunteers,
40   who mumbled their thanks as they tried to shield the donuts from the water.

"Just another reason I never want to see this crummy place again," Jesse muttered to himself as he helped hand out coffee day after day. "What kind of a place is this, anyway? Floods, mudslides. Stupid."

The water kept rising. On the third day, the volunteers had to scramble to
45   avoid the rising water, and they **abandoned** the effort to keep back the flood.

Jesse and his dad ran to the store, realizing that the water was headed to the low-lying downtown streets. **Frantically,** they tried to get as much merchandise as they could off the floor. Finally, a couple of firefighters had to pull them out of the store as a roaring wave escaped the river banks and rushed down the street in front
50   of their store.

Helplessly, Jesse and his dad watched from a higher area as the water settled on the street as if it were the river's natural course. Out of the corner of his eye, Jesse watched his dad's eyes shine with tears that he roughly brushed away.

Jesse's dad turned to his son. "To you, this may be a horrible place. For me, it's
55   been my life," he said in a choked voice. Then he turned to walk home. Jesse followed.

2. Do you think Jesse and his father are getting emotionally closer or further apart because of the storm? Why do you think so?

_____

_____

merchandise *(noun)*
   things for sale, such
   as groceries

The store is flooded. Make a prediction about what will happen next at the store. Read on to find out if your prediction is correct.

The downtown area was the hardest hit. After the river **receded,** the retailers came back, armed with buckets and mops and rags. Jesse and his dad and the rest of the family came, too. Without saying much, they began the painful job of cleaning up the muck, making piles of ruined merchandise. Jesse was so busy
60   he didn't notice that before long there were others working with them. Dozens of people came armed with mops they had brought from home. Jesse's father looked up in surprise, too.

"Of course we'd come to help," said one heavy older man gruffly, putting his mop into the mud that remained. "You're part of us. We need you here."
65   "Remember when you gave me credit for six months when my Opie lost his job?" said one woman. "I'll never forget." She turned back to her mop.

"I remember stealing candy in here when I was a kid," grinned a skinny twenty-something guy. "I figure I owe you." A burst of laughter rolled through the volunteers at the store.
70   Rene shook his finger in mock sternness. "You think I didn't see you?" he said. Jesse joined in the laughter as he mopped.

For four days, the customers came back, lugging their mops and buckets, washing and restocking the shelves. At the end, the place looked presentable again. In fact, it looked great. Rene and Jesse brought over a barbecue grill and
75   cooked hamburgers for everyone.

Every bit of his body ached, Jesse thought as he bit into a burger. He looked at the group gathered around the grill. Mrs. McNeely was playfully feeling the muscles in Jesse's friend Dominic's arm. His father hugged tiny Mr. Herredia as they both laughed. Jesse's mom was squirting ketchup in a smiley face on a kid's
80   hamburger.

Thoughtfully, Jesse ate, watching these people he'd known his whole life. A feeling of goodwill **permeated** the store and its still-muddy sidewalk. He could leave, but maybe this was what everyone left to search for—a community of people who cared and whom you cared about. Maybe this was his life, the days of
85   small change and small jokes, and that was OK. Maybe he was fine right here.

retailers (noun)
people who sell goods in a store

3. Were you surprised that Jesse changed his mind about his future after the flood? Why or why not?

_____

_____

4. Do you think that Jesse will be content in this community forever, or for a while, or will he change his mind again? Why do you think so?

_____

_____

After You Read

Build a robust vocabulary.

Writing Sentences   Write a complete sentence to respond to each of the following questions or statements. Use the underlined word in your answer. Use the definitions on page 35 to help you.

1. How would you meticulously keep a budget?

    _____

2. How many generations are still alive in your family?

    _____

3. After a big rainstorm, what might be permeated with water?

    _____

4. What can you do when someone has a tantrum?

    _____

5. What is the season preceding spring?

    _____

Sentence Completions   Complete each sentence using a word from the box.

abandoned	frantically	generations	horizontally	meticulously
permeated	preceding	receded	tantrum	torrent

1. The family _____ their flooded and ruined house.

2. I held in my anger for a long time, but it finally came out in a _____ of words.

3. The water finally _____ and the street was no longer a river.

4. The family tried _____ to stop the water from entering their home.

5. The rain was blown _____ by the wind.

Word Building   When you show an action that happened in the past, you use the **past tense**. Often you add *-ed* to the end of the action word, or verb. For example, the word *walk* becomes *walked*, and the word *wash* becomes *washed*. If there is an *e* on the end of the verb, you add only *d,* as in *race* and *raced*.

Sometimes you need to make spelling changes when you write the past form of a verb. You double the *p* when you want to change *skip* to *skipped*. If the last syllable of the word has a short vowel (for example, the *i* in *skip*), double the last letter. *Pat* becomes *patted*, and *stop* becomes *stopped*.

Read these past tense verbs. Circle the -d or -ed endings. Underline the letters that were doubled to make the past tense. Then write a sentence using the past form of each verb.

1. jumped: _____

2. cleaned: _____

3. hiked: _____

4. flipped: _____

5. stapled: _____

6. washed: _____

TIP: Sometimes there is no pattern to forming the past tense of the verb. You just have to know the word. What is the past form of *run?* It's *ran.* What is the past form of *write?* It's *wrote.*

Writing Activity   Write a short paragraph that correctly uses key vocabulary words to tell about the storm in the story. Use at least four of the words from the list on page 35. Reread the definitions, if necessary.

_____

_____

_____

_____

Think about your reading.

Check your comprehension.   Answer each question. If you don't know the answer, reread the lines in parentheses.

1. What is the routine at the store every evening? (lines 3–5)

_____

2. What are the sandbags for? (lines 34–38)

_____

3. Why do Jesse and his father rush to the store during the storm? (lines 46–48)

_____

4. Why do people come to help Jesse and his father at the store? (lines 63–69)

_____

Use reading skills: Identify cause and effect.

When you identify cause and effect, you notice how one event makes another event happen. The **cause** is what makes something happen. The **effect** is what happens as a result. You see examples of this every day. You might feel cold air. You see the window is open. The open window is the cause. The effect is you feel the cold air.

Identify cause and effect. In the first part of the story, you find out that Jesse isn't happy.

1. Jesse being unhappy is the _____

2. The fact that he doesn't want to work there is the _____

Reread this section from the story:

> "I remember stealing candy in here when I was a kid," grinned a skinny twenty-something guy. "I figure I owe you." A burst of laughter rolled through the volunteers at the store.

3. The young man stole candy from the store when he was a kid. What is the effect of that?

_____

_____

Use a graphic organizer.

Fill in the missing cause and effect in the boxes below to understand the events that happen in the story.

Causes	Effects
1.	Volunteers abandon the effort to keep back the water with sandbags.
Customers of the store feel that Jesse's dad has helped them out over the years.	2.

Write About It

Write a story summary.

A summary includes the most important parts of a story or an article. In a summary, you leave out the details that are not important to understanding the main idea of the story. For example, in a summary of this story, you would probably leave out how Jesse and his father close up the store every night. Write a summary of "After the Storm."

Prewriting   Stories have important events that happen in a particular order. A graphic organizer can help you remember the important events and when they happened. Then you can use your organizer to help you write your summary. Fill in the important events of the story. The first one is written for you.

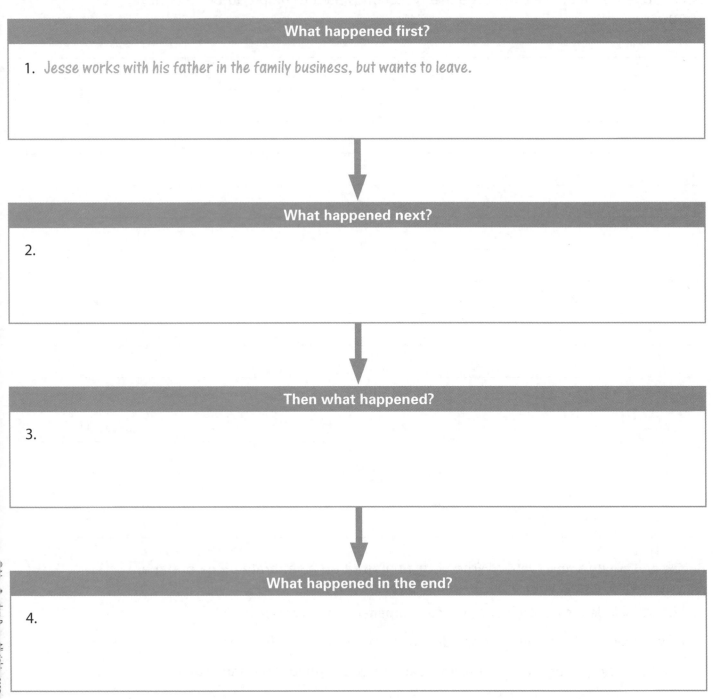

What happened first?

1. Jesse works with his father in the family business, but wants to leave.

What happened next?

2.

Then what happened?

3.

What happened in the end?

4.

Thinking Beyond Reading   Think about these questions and discuss them with a partner. Add ideas to the graphic organizer as you talk.

- What events are most important in the story?

- How would you feel if you were in Jesse's shoes?

- How is the store important to the community?

- How does Jesse think differently about the store after the storm?

Write a draft.   Write a first draft of your summary paragraph. Make sure you include the important events that happened in the story. You might begin your summary with a topic sentence like this: "Jesse works in his family's business, but he really isn't happy about it." Use the organizer you completed to help you write your summary.

_____

_____

_____

_____

_____

_____

_____

_____

_____

_____

_____

_____

_____

Revise and create a final draft.   Write your final draft on a separate piece of paper. As you revise, check your draft for these specific points:

- Did you include the important events that happened, in the correct order?

- Did you make sure that unimportant ideas or events are not in your summary?

- Did you check spelling and grammar to make sure your writing is clear and correct?

Read All About It

Learning Objectives

In this lesson you will:

▓ Read about a man who learned to read as an adult

▓ Learn to identify words that show time order.

▓ Master the key vocabulary used in the article.

▓ Write directions telling a child how to get ready for school.

Key Vocabulary

agency *(noun)* a business that provides a particular service

bruised *(adjective)* wounded or hurt

embarrassed *(adjective)* uncomfortable, especially in front of other people

emotionally *(adverb)* with feelings

gifted *(adjective)* having a natural talent for doing something well

humiliation *(noun)* shame

invested *(verb)* paid out money in order to make a profit

manual *(noun)* a book that gives instructions

ridiculed *(verb)* made fun of

submit *(verb)* to hand in

Before You Read

As you begin to read the article, you will see that it is about John Corcoran, a man who couldn't read. You can ask yourself this question: What do I already know about this problem? You can also try to predict what you will read about. These active reading strategies will help you better comprehend what you read.

Use what you know.

1. What problems have you or has someone you know had in school?

   _____

   _____

   _____

2. What did you do or your friend do to fix the problem?

   _____

   _____

   _____

3. What other types of school problems have you heard about?

   _____

   _____

   _____

Make predictions while you read.

1. Why do you think John Corcoran hid the fact that he couldn't read?

   _____

   _____

   _____

2. Do you think someone can do well in business if he or she can't read? Why or why not?

   _____

   _____

   _____

It's Never too Late

Read the story to find out how John Corcoran got through school. Use a sticky note to keep track of things he did to get by.

Imagine that you're a student in a welding class. Your teacher asks you to read the first few paragraphs of a **manual** silently, and then discuss it with a partner. You stare at the page. But all you see is a lot of letters, spaces, and dots. You don't see words.

5 You don't want to be **ridiculed.** So you try to fake it. Since the topic is welding, you think that the page probably has to do with heating metal pieces. Your heart beats fast. In a minute, your partner will look up, ready to discuss what he read. But you have to pretend you read the paragraphs because you can't read well.

10 For most of his life, that's the way John Corcoran felt whenever he had to read a manual, a letter, a street sign, a newspaper article, or a job application. In spite of years of **humiliation** as a poor reader, he was a very successful businessman. So successful that he became a multimillionaire. But the fact that he couldn't read never stopped bothering him.

15 So one day when he was 48, Corcoran walked into a tutoring **agency** and spoke the words he had kept secret for most of his life. "I can't read."

welding (verb)
joining metal parts by heating

1. Why was what John said when he was 48 so surprising?

_____

_____

Continue reading to learn how John got by in school. Underline sentences that tell how scared he was that others would learn his secret.

The Problem Begins

John Corcoran grew up in Santa Fe, New Mexico. He was **gifted** in sports. He smashed home runs with his baseball bat, kicked touchdowns on the
20 football field, and tore up the dirt roads on his bike.

But inside the classroom, life was not as easy for him. While the other kids were learning that c-a-t read *cat*, John simply stared at the page. He didn't know that letters have sounds and that letters and sounds form words. He didn't know how to sound out words or to figure them out from the rest of the story.
25 John hated school because he couldn't keep up. But he never told anyone he couldn't read. He thought it was his fault. One day was especially painful, **emotionally** and physically. His teacher told the class to complete a workbook page. John wanted to do it, but he couldn't. So he sat quietly at his desk. The teacher got angry, thinking John was just being difficult. The teacher asked John
30 to read aloud. John was silent. "Roll up your pants," his teacher said. Each kid in John's row used the teacher's yardstick to hit John's leg. John returned to his seat at the back of the room, **bruised** in more ways than one. From that day on, he decided that he would never again be **embarrassed** because he couldn't read.

2. In what ways was John bruised when the teacher had other students hit him on the leg?

_____

_____

3. What questions do you have about John's problem? Do you think your questions will be answered in the rest of the article? Explain.

_____

_____

Finish reading to find out how John solved his problems.

High School and Beyond

35 John tried faking, lying, and cheating. Throughout junior high and high school, he listened to discussions in class to guess what was written in textbooks. In junior college, his girlfriend helped him out. When he had a paper to **submit,** he told her what he wanted to say and she typed it for him. Sometimes he bought essays from other students or from professional writers.
40 Towards the end of junior college, John even stole in order to hide his secret. It was right before a big test. John knew he couldn't read the exam

questions, so he broke into the teacher's office and stole a file cabinet. He asked a friend to find the exam he needed. Then he returned the file cabinet.

Professional Life

45 Incredibly, after graduation, John applied for a job as a teacher. Still unable to read, John had his father fill out the application for him. He got the teaching job. He also became a coach. When he was in the classroom, John asked his students to read aloud. They had no idea that he was probably the only one in the room who couldn't read.

50 Years later he went into real estate. He became an expert in the California real estate market. He bought and sold properties, making huge profits. He **invested** in the market and the investments paid off. He made millions. He got married and had kids.

Then one day when he was 48, John walked into a tutoring agency and 55 asked a teacher for one-on-one instruction. Over time, he learned to read. "It was like a whole new world opened up to me," Corcoran said.

Corcoran got the help he needed and learned to read. But he did far more than that. He talked to local community groups about his experience. He spoke to millions on TV. He met with the President at the White House. He 60 wrote *The Teacher Who Couldn't Read*.

The more he traveled, the more Corcoran realized how many Americans were illiterate. He started a foundation to end illiteracy in the United States. Today he is head of the John Corcoran Foundation. The foundation gives money to programs that teach reading to children and adults across the 65 country. John Corcoran doesn't want anyone else to share his experience as a non-reader. John Corcoran has made a difference.

profits (noun)
  gains, usually in money

foundation (noun)
  an organization that supports a cause

illiteracy (noun)
  the condition of not being able to read or write

4. Do you think that illiteracy is a big problem in the United States?

_____

_____

5. In your experience, did Corcoran take the right steps to fix the problem? Why or why not?

_____

_____

6. What questions do you still have about Corcoran's story? Try to figure out the answers based on what you know.

_____

_____

After You Read

Build a robust vocabulary.

Writing Sentences   Write a complete sentence to respond to each of the following questions or statements. Use the underlined word in your answer. Use the definitions on page 45 to help you.

1.   Tell about a time you saw someone being <u>ridiculed</u>.

_____

2.   When was the last time you were <u>embarrassed</u>?

_____

3.   How do you feel when you're <u>bruised</u>?

_____

4.   In what ways was John Corcoran <u>gifted</u>?

_____

5.   When have you had to use a <u>manual</u>?

_____

Sentence Completions   Complete each sentence using a word from the box.

agency	bruised	embarrassed	emotionally	gifted
humiliation	invested	manual	ridiculed	submit

1.   Ava felt great _____ because she couldn't read.

2.   When Maria saw the sad movie, she reacted _____.

3.   I went to an employment _____ to look for a job.

4.   The students have to _____ their papers on Monday.

5.   We _____ our money in a savings account at the bank.

Word Building   Plurals are words that mean *more than one*. If a person, place, or thing ends with -*s,* the -*s* often makes the word mean "more than one." If a person, place, or thing ends with -*x, -s, -ch, -sh,* or -*ss,* you add -*es* to form the plural. For example *brush* becomes *brushes.* If a person, place, or thing ends with *y,* you usually change -*y* to -*i* and add -*es.* For example, *activity* becomes *activities.*

Look at the following words. What is the same about all of them?

schools	lunches	teachers	pennies

All of the words are plural. Circle the letters that make them plural. Compare your answers with a partner. Discuss what each word means.

Read the following words. Write the plural form of each word. The first one is done for you.

1. property: _properties_ _____

2. sign: _____

3. letter: _____

4. coach: _____

5. agency: _____

Write two sentences. Use one of the plural words above in each sentence.

6. _____

7. _____

TIP: When you read, you may find words that end in *s* that you do not know. Look at the rest of the word. Is it a person, place, or thing? Does it end with *-s, -es,* or *-ies?* Then decide if the word means more than one thing.

Writing Activity   Write a short paragraph that correctly uses key vocabulary words to tell about a school problem you or a friend once had. Use at least four of the words from the list on page 45. Reread the definitions, if necessary.

_____

_____

_____

_____

Think about your reading.

Check your comprehension.   Answer each question. If you don't know the answer, reread the lines in parentheses.

1. What kinds of things did John Corcoran have trouble reading? (lines 10–11)

_____

2. What did he say when he entered the tutoring agency? (lines 15–16)

_____

3. Why did he keep silent about his problem? (line 26)

_____

4. How did his father help him get a job? (lines 45–46)

_____

Use reading skills: Identify time order words.

Articles and stories are sometimes arranged in **time order.** When you read, you note what happens first, next, and last. Some words that give clues to time order are *first, second, then, later, next, last, finally, before, after, today,* and *at the end.*

Identify time order words.   Read the following sentences from the article. Each sentence contains one or more words that tell when an event happened. Underline those words in each sentence.

1.   Towards the end of junior college, John even stole to hide his secret.

2.   Then he returned the file cabinet.

3.   Incredibly, after graduation, John applied for a job as a teacher.

4.   Years later, he went into real estate.

5.   Today he is head of the John Corcoran Foundation.

Use a graphic organizer.

Read the short passage below. Fill in the chart below. Write Emily's story in correct time order. Use words such as *first, second, then, later, next, last, finally, before, after, today,* and *at the end.*

Emily decided she needed help. She found a program that provides tutoring. She called them. She told the tutor, "I can't read." The tutor taught Emily to read.

Emily Makes a Change
1. Last year Emily decided she needed help.
2.
3.
4.
5.

Write About It

Write directions.

Your seven-year-old son doesn't get ready for school on time. He's always late. Make a list of directions that will help him be on time. Write the directions in time order.

Prewriting   On your own or with a partner, write a list of things that your son needs to do to get ready for school. Then number the steps in time order. Use the graphic organizer to put your ideas in order. Add more lines if you need them.

Order	How to Get Ready for School

Thinking Beyond Reading   Think about these questions and discuss them with a partner. Add ideas to the graphic organizer as you talk. Then do the same for your partner.

- What do you do before you get dressed?

- What is the first thing you do to get dressed?

- What do you do next?

- What comes last?

Write a draft.   Write a first draft paragraph that tells your seven-year-old son how to get ready for school. Your paragraph might begin with this topic sentence: "To get ready for school on time, first. . . ." Use the details in your chart to complete your paragraph. Add as many details as you can.

_____

_____

_____

_____

_____

_____

_____

_____

_____

_____

_____

_____

_____

_____

_____

_____

Revise and create a final draft.   Write your final draft on a separate piece of paper. As you revise, check your draft for these specific points:

- Did you write the steps in time order?

- Did you include time order words?

- Did you check spelling and grammar to make sure your writing is clear and correct?

Hard Work Pays Off

Learning Objectives

In this lesson you will:

▧ Learn about a Congresswoman from Florida.

▧ Learn to make judgments about information.

▧ Master the key vocabulary used in the article.

▧ Write a letter to the editor.

Key Vocabulary

achievers *(noun)* people who carry things out successfully

diversity *(noun)* variety

evicted *(verb)* forced to leave a rental property

fluent *(adjective)* capable of using a language easily and accurately

immigration *(noun)* the process of coming to live in a new country

mission *(noun)* a special job given to a person or a group of people

objectives *(noun)* aims or goals

obstacles *(noun)* things that get in the way

persistence *(noun)* continuing to do something in a firm, steady way; not giving up

violence *(noun)* actions that intend to cause injury, pain, or harm

Before You Read

As you read the article, you will find out about a woman who came to the United States as a child, without knowing any English, and who became a successful U.S. Congresswoman. Think about what it would be like to live in a country without being able to speak the language used there.

Use what you know.

1. Do you know people in the United States who do not speak English? What languages do they speak?

   _____

   _____

   _____

2. How do these people manage at home, in the neighborhood, and at work?

   _____

   _____

   _____

3. What problems do non-English speakers sometimes have in school?

   _____

   _____

   _____

Preview the article.

1. Look at the picture on page 57. What does it tell you about the article?

   _____

   _____

   _____

2. Read the title of the article. What language besides English do you see?

   _____

   _____

   _____

THINK ABOUT IT

My friend came to this country in first grade. He couldn't speak English. At first, he had no one at school to talk to. It's hard when you don't know English.

THINK ABOUT IT

I see a woman standing in front of a flag. The article must be about her.

Hola, Congresswoman!

Read the following article to find out about a Congresswoman from Florida. Jot down on sticky notes what you think is interesting about her.

If you put a sign in your house telling visitors what's important to you, what would it say? I love dogs? Let's Go Mets? Music Rules?

If you asked Florida Congresswoman Ileana Ros-Lehtinen the same question, her response would probably be, "**Persistence** counts." That's because
5 Ros-Lehtinen is a woman who has lived her life with determination. She has the ability to stick to a task, even in the face of **obstacles.** She fights for things that are important to her. That has helped her reach her goals. She became the first female Hispanic in Congress. She has used her position to fight for women's rights and the environment . She also serves as a role model for
10 Hispanic women and men everywhere.

But to understand Ros-Lehtinen, it's important to know what a member of Congress does.

A Varied Job

Members of Congress have several responsibilities. First, they represent the
15 people from their districts . Ros-Lehtinen, for example, represents a district in south Florida. Sixty-seven percent of her district is Hispanic.

Members of Congress vote on many different issues, from education to health care. As they vote on a bill, they think of their constituents' views as well as their own views—and the country as a whole. These
20 votes are important. With enough votes, a bill may become law. Although Congresspeople come from different states, they all work together in Washington, DC. They often go home on weekends so they can stay in touch with people there. As Ros-Lehtinen once told a reporter, "I enjoy the people

environment *(noun)*
the natural world of the land, sea, and air

Congress *(noun)*
the part of the U. S. government that makes laws

district *(noun)*
an area or region

constituents *(noun)*
voters who choose an elected official

legislative *(adjective)*
of or about making laws

25 contact as much as the legislative part of my job. Many of the issues I'm involved with were brought to my attention by my constituents."

1. What special qualities does the Congresswoman have?

_____

_____

2. What issues does the Congresswoman fight for?

_____

_____

Continue reading the article to find out more about the Congresswoman's life and work.

Second, a Congresswoman tries to solve people's problems. Perhaps a man is separated from his family because of **immigration** rules. Maybe a woman is being **evicted** from her apartment unfairly. Problems vary. But the job of the Congressperson is to make things right. Members of Congress get thousands 30 of letters and phone calls each year from people who need help.

Congress is divided into two branches, the House of Representatives and the Senate. There are 535 members in all. Ileana Ros-Lehtinen is one of 435 members who come from the House of Representatives. One hundred members come from the Senate.

35 **Early Years**

At the age of seven, Ileana Ros-Lehtinen arrived in the United States from Havana, Cuba. "I came without knowing a word of English," Ros-Lehtinen remembers. Yet she quickly learned English. She set goals to become **fluent** and to help people. She rose through the school system. She earned a doctorate 40 degree in education from a university in Miami.

Then she became a teacher. Before long, she heard about a small private school near Miami. Passionate about education, she got a job there as principal. She led the school for nine years. In 1989, after other political jobs, she ran for election to the House of Representatives—and she won!

45 It wasn't easy. As a Hispanic woman, she faced resistance, but she overcame doubters who questioned her ability. Said Ros-Lehtinen, "I concentrated on my **mission** and my **objectives.** I didn't worry about other people's doubts." She had a tough race but she only looked ahead.

In many ways, her success is related to a strong work ethic. Her assistant 50 said the Congresswoman "always returns phone calls and is never late for anything."

3. How did Ros-Lehtinen show persistence?

_____

_____

4. How did she show a strong work ethic?

_____

_____

Finish reading the article. Mark information that tells you about the things the Congresswoman does.

The votes that a Congresswoman casts are important. They show things she feels strongly about. Ros-Lehtinen has done many things to further women's rights. She supports programs that address **violence** toward women.
55 She also gets funding for people with breast cancer. In addition, Ros-Lehtinen said, "I always make an effort to speak to young women." She gets their views about what needs to be done to help them, and she encourages them "to become involved in their communities."
When it comes to the environment, Ros-Lehtinen has voted to protect
60 Florida's coastline. She also fights for money to clean up the Miami River.
It is important to Ros-Lehtinen that she is a role model for Hispanics. She wants other Hispanics to strive to reach their goals. Ros-Lehtinen is especially aware of the **diversity** among Hispanic women. She says, a Hispanic woman can be any number of things. "A writer. Or a computer programmer. Or an
65 attorney. Or a doctor. As well as a loving wife and mother." In other words, Ileana Ros-Lehtinen believes that Hispanic women can be high **achievers** in all areas of life.
Ros-Lehtinen knows what it takes for all people to succeed: Set goals. Work hard. Keep high standards. Believe in yourself. And above all, show
70 persistence. Like Ros-Lehtinen herself.

5. Do you think the Congresswoman is a role model? Why or why not?

_____

_____

6. Do you think the Congresswoman is determined to help people? What makes you think so?

_____

_____

After You Read

Build a robust vocabulary.

Writing Sentences Write a complete sentence to respond to each of the following questions or statements. Use the underlined word in your answer. Use the definitions on page 55 to help you.

1. Tell about a time you saw <u>diversity</u> in a group of people.

    _____

2. Do you know anyone who has gone through the <u>immigration</u> process?

    _____

3. What happens when someone is <u>evicted</u> from their home?

    _____

4. Tell about a time you showed <u>persistence</u> in getting something done.

    _____

5. What <u>obstacles</u> might keep you from achieving your goals?

    _____

Sentence Completions Complete each sentence using a word from the box.

achievers	diversity	evicted	fluent	immigration
mission	objectives	obstacles	persistence	violence

1. When Lily came to America, she was not _____ in English.

2. When you set goals for yourself, you have _____.

3. People who get all As in school are high _____.

4. John's _____ in life is to become a teacher.

5. Many people believe that children should not see _____ on TV or in the movies.

Word Building A **root word** is the main part of a word. It holds most of the word's meaning. An example of a root word is *agree,* meaning "to have the same opinion."

Sometimes a part is added to the beginning of a root word. The prefix *dis-* added to the root word *agree* makes *disagree,* which means "not to have the same opinion."

At other times, a part is added to the end of the root word. The suffix *-ment* is added to the root word *agree* to make *agreement,* which means "the act or result of having the same opinion."

Each of the words below has a root word and a prefix or suffix. Circle the part of each word that is the root. Use the meaning of the root word and the meaning of the prefix or suffix to help you figure out what each word means. Then write another word with the same root. The first one is done for you.

1. election: _elected_ _____

2. return: _____

3. evicted: _____

4. funding: _____

5. strongly: _____

TIP: Recognizing the root word within a word can help you understand the word's meaning. Look for the root word in a long or difficult word to help you figure out its meaning.

Writing Activity   Write a short paragraph that correctly uses key vocabulary words to tell about a politician you know of or would like to learn about. Use at least four of the words from the list on page 55. Reread the definitions, if necessary.

_____

_____

_____

_____

Think about your reading.

Check your comprehension.   Answer each question. If you don't know the answer, reread the lines in parentheses.

1. In what state is the district Congresswoman Ros-Lehtinen represents? (lines 15–16)

_____

2. What is one responsibility of a member of Congress? (lines 14–18)

_____

3. From which country did Ros-Lehtinen originally come to the United States? (lines 36–37)

_____

4. What has Congresswoman Ros-Lehtinen done to support women's health issues? (lines 53–55)

_____

5. What has Congresswoman Ros-Lehtinen done to help the environment? (lines 59–60)

_____

Use reading skills: Make judgments.

As you read, you **make judgments** about the actions of the person in the article. You make those judgments by combining what the author said with your own experiences.

Make judgments. In the article, we learn about Ros-Lehtinen's actions in Congress. Read the following sentences from the article.

> Ros-Lehtinen has done many things to further women's rights. She supports programs that address violence toward women. She also gets funding for people with breast cancer.

1. What issue does the Congresswoman feel strongly about?

   _____

2. Why would a person who supports women's rights also support programs against violence toward women?

   _____

3. Do you think Ros-Lehtinen fights for women's rights?

   _____

Use a graphic organizer.

These graphic organizers can help you make judgments. Use the ideas in the article and your own experience. Fill in the missing information in the charts below.

What the article says	Ros-Lehtinen supports women's rights.
What I know	1.
My judgment	2.

What the article says	It is important to Ros-Lehtinen that she is a role model for Hispanics.
What I know	3.
My judgment	4.

Write About It

Write a letter to the editor.

You read an editorial in your local newspaper. It is in favor of opening a large cement plant near where you live. Write a letter to the editor saying why you agree or disagree with that editorial.

> The cement plant should be allowed to open up in our area. It will bring lots of new jobs to the area. It will bring in other new businesses, like coffee shops and dry cleaners. If the dust from the plant gets into our air and water, we can clean it up later. If people get dust in their lungs, they can visit a doctor. The environment can wait. Our health will be fine. We need jobs and money now.

Prewriting   On your own or with a partner, jot down ideas in the editorial, ideas from your own experience, and your judgment about the issue. Use your notes to write the letter. Fill in the graphic organizer to help you plan your letter.

What the editorial says	
What I know	
My judgment about the editorial	
More reasons to support my judgment	

Thinking Beyond Reading   Think about these ideas and discuss them with a partner. Add ideas to the graphic organizer as you talk.

- Why and how would a new plant create jobs?

- How would a new plant bring in other businesses, such as coffee shops?

- How do you feel about the effects of the plant on the environment?

Write a draft.   Write a first draft of your letter. Include details from the editorial, your own experience, and your overall judgment. Start your letter by stating your judgment. For example, "To the Editor: The proposed cement plant will (or will not) be good for our area." Then give reasons to support your point of view.

_____

_____

_____

_____

_____

_____

_____

_____

_____

_____

_____

_____

_____

_____

_____

_____

Revise and create a final draft.   Write your final draft on a separate piece of paper. As you revise, check your draft for these specific points:

- Did you state your judgment at the beginning of the letter?

- Did you include reasons for your judgment?

- Is your letter based on statements in the editorial as well as your own experience?

- Did you check spelling and grammar to make sure your writing is clear and correct?

Everyone's a Winner

Learning Objectives

In this lesson you will:

■ Read a story about two brothers and their favorite sports.

■ Learn to compare and contrast ideas.

■ Master the key vocabulary used in the story.

■ Write a recommendation.

Key Vocabulary

avid *(adjective)* very eager

determined *(adjective)* having a strong desire to do something even if it is difficult

draped *(adjective)* hanging loosely

dully *(adverb)* without interest

elated *(adjective)* extremely happy and excited

enthusiastic *(adjective)* showing a lot of excitement about something

intense *(adjective)* extreme

self-portrait *(noun)* a picture you make of yourself

settle *(verb)* to end an argument

strategy *(noun)* a careful plan or method

Before You Read

As you begin to read the story about two brothers, you will find out which sport each one prefers. Try using these active reading strategies to find out more about the brothers. Use what you know by thinking about sports that you like and preview the story by looking at the picture and the title.

Use what you know.

THINK ABOUT IT

My favorite sport is basketball. I watch professional and college ball on TV. Sometimes I go to the park and watch the kids play.

1. Do you have a favorite sport to watch? What sport is it?

   _____

   _____

   _____

2. Why do you like that sport?

   _____

   _____

   _____

3. Do you know people who prefer a different sport? Which sport is that?

   _____

   _____

   _____

Preview the story.

THINK ABOUT IT

It looks to me like the brothers are arguing. One looks like he's ready to play baseball. The other is watching basketball on TV.

1. Read the title of the story. What does it tell you?

   _____

   _____

   _____

2. Look at the picture on page 67. What does it show you?

   _____

   _____

   _____

Score!

Read the story to find out why two brothers disagree about sports. Mark phrases that show how the sports are different.

"Aw, c'mon. Shoot the ball! Shoot the ball!" 23-year-old Matt shouts at the TV set, as he leaps from the living room couch to yell at the player on the screen. "Take the shot," Matt shouts, throwing an imaginary ball into a hoop.

"What's going on?" his twin brother Ricky calls from the kitchen.

5 "Come in here. Bailey just made the most amazing shot. Hurry!"

"Hold on," Ricky says **dully.** "I'm making a sandwich."

"Come now. Watch the replay."

"Nah," says Ricky. "You know basketball's not my game."

It's halftime now. The twin brothers' five-year-old nephew, Angelo, enters the 10 living room. Angelo is playing a video game, which pings and beeps.

Ricky enters the living room, too. He's wearing a baseball jersey and baseball cap. "You're too into basketball," Ricky tells his brother. "I'd much rather watch a baseball game. There's more **strategy** in baseball."

"Are you kidding me?" Matt replies. "Basketball's full of strategy. Who's going 15 to pass? Who's going to take the shot? Basketball is all about strategy."

"Sure," Ricky counters. "But in baseball the players are a team. What one man does affects the others. Remember last week's game? Phillips sees three men on base. You know that he's going to hit a grounder so that the guy on third base will come in. And score! Like I said, teamwork."

1. Which of the two games, baseball and basketball, do you prefer? Why?

_____

_____

2. Do you think the two brothers respect each other's opinions? Explain.

_____

_____

Continue reading the story to find out how the brothers plan to end their argument. Mark sentences that show their differences.

20   "It's the same thing with basketball," says Matt. "It's a team sport, too. But it's more exciting," he adds. "More **intense.**"

"No way! Baseball's the game to watch. Right, Angelo?"

"Huh?" replies the boy.

"Which do you prefer? Basketball or baseball?"

25   "Prefer?" says Angelo.

"Yeah. You know. Which is better? More exciting?"

"Um. I don't know," Angelo answers.

And that's when the two brothers decide to put their favorite games to a test. They agree to take their nephew—who has never been to a game before—to a

30   basketball game and a baseball game. Angelo will **settle** the debate. He'll draw a picture of what he likes about each sport and decide which is "best."

The next day the three set out for a basketball game. **Determined** to win the argument, Matt points out the strengths of basketball to his nephew. And Matt explains the rules. Angelo keeps a notepad and a pencil on his lap.

35   Matt begins, "There are two teams, see?" Matt says, putting his arm around the boy's shoulder and pointing to the action on the court.

"The guys in red are on one team and the guys in blue are on the other. Each time a player gets a ball in the basket, he scores two points. If he shoots behind the line, he gets three points. The winner is the team with the most points when

40   the final buzzer sounds."

"OK," says Angelo. "That sounds easy."

"Not really. The other team tries to stop them from scoring by guarding or stealing the ball. I'll explain about passing and dribbling later. And about offensive and defensive strategies. The game is played in four quarters, each

45   12 minutes. Each team works together to score points."

"All right," Angelo says, absorbing the information. "But who's that man over there? In the suit. On the side," asks Angelo.

"That's the coach. He tells the players what to do."

Matt cheers each time his team scores. Soon Angelo is cheering with him.

50   The game ends. Matt's team won. Matt leaves **elated.**

"Exciting, huh?" says Matt. He ruffles his nephew's hair.

3. Do you think Angelo understands the game? How can you tell?

_____

_____

dribbling (verb)
    moving a ball forward
    by bouncing it

offensive (adjective)
    related to trying to
    score in a sport

defensive (adjective)
    related to trying to
    stop the other team
    from scoring

ruffles (verb)
    disturbs the surface of

4. How do you think Ricky feels about Matt's explanation of basketball?

_____

_____

Finish reading the story. As you read, stop every so often and summarize Ricky's reaction to baseball.

The next day the three go to a baseball game. Now it's Ricky's turn to point out the beauty of *his* game.

"So," Ricky begins, putting his arm around Angelo's shoulder.

55 "Baseball's got two teams, too, the guys in blue and the guys in red. Each team has nine players, not five. See their ball?"

"Yeah," says Angelo. "It's smaller than a basketball."

"Right. Smaller and harder. Plus, they use a bat. The team that's up tries to score a run by hitting the ball and running around the bases, called a diamond.

60 There are nine innings ."

"Does a buzzer go off at the end?" asks Angelo.

"No, it's not timed. The team with the most runs after nine innings wins. They take turns. Three outs and the next team goes."

The guys watch the game. Ricky pounds his chest when his team gets a run.

65 "Who's that man over there?" asks Angelo.

"That's the coach. He teaches strategy and decides on the lineup—which guys play. I'll explain about defensive strategies later." Ricky ruffles his nephew's hair.

Ricky's team wins the game, 8–6. Ricky is excited and punches the air. He's an **avid** fan. Matt enjoys the game, too, but he's not as **enthusiastic** as his brother.

70 The three arrive home. It's late. "So Angelo, which game is more exciting?" the men ask.

But Angelo has already fallen asleep on the couch. The men pick up Angelo's pad. There, in the middle of the page, is a **self-portrait** of Angelo. His hair is ruffled. Uncle Matt's arm is **draped** over the boy's left shoulder and Uncle Ricky's

75 arm is draped over the right. The boy in the picture has a broad grin on his face.

The men laugh and then head to the kitchen for a snack.

innings *(noun)*
the playing periods in a baseball game

5. Do you think Angelo will like sports when he grows up? Why or why not?

_____

_____

6. Why do you think Angelo drew the picture the way he did? What does that tell you about his experiences with his uncles?

_____

_____

After You Read

Build a robust vocabulary.

Writing Sentences Write a complete sentence to respond to each of the following questions or statements. Use the underlined word in your answer. Use the definitions on page 65 to help you.

1. Tell about a time you had to <u>settle</u> an argument for someone.

    _____

2. What sports are you <u>enthusiastic</u> about?

    _____

3. Tell about one <u>strategy</u> for having a successful life.

    _____

4. Do you think basketball is a more <u>intense</u> sport than golf?

    _____

5. Name something you are <u>determined</u> to do?

    _____

Sentence Completions Complete each sentence using a word from the box.

avid	determined	draped	dully	elated
enthusiastic	intense	self-portrait	settle	strategy

1. Lucia loves the outdoors and is an _____ gardener.

2. Kathy was so _____ by the good news that she jumped up and down.

3. I had to draw my _____ in art class last night.

4. Vincent spoke _____ about the boring movie.

5. Matt's basketball jersey is _____ over the back of the chair.

Word Building   Compound words are words made of two or more smaller words. You can often tell the meaning of a compound word by looking for the two smaller words. *Armchair, fireplace, sunset,* and *haircut* are all compound words.

Read this sentence from the story.

> He teaches strategy and decides on the lineup—which guys play.

There is one compound word in the sentence. It is *lineup.* Draw a line between the two smaller words in *lineup.* Check your answer with a partner.

Read these compound words. What is the same about all of them?

underpaid	undershirt	underweight	undercooked

All of the words begin with *under*. Write two sentences. Use one of the words above in each sentence.

1. _____

2. _____

TIP: When you read, you may find some long words you do not know. Does the word have two words combined to make one word? Look closely to see if the word is a compound word.

Writing Activity   Write a short paragraph that correctly uses key vocabulary words to tell about watching a game you really like. Use at least four of the words from the list on page 65. Reread the definitions, if necessary.

_____

_____

_____

_____

_____

Think about your reading.

Check your comprehension.   Answer each question. If you don't know the answer, reread the lines in parentheses.

1. How do Ricky's clothes show his favorite sport? (lines 11–12)

_____

2. What game did the brothers take Angelo to first? (line 32)

_____

3. What game did the brothers take Angelo to next? (line 52)

_____

4. When they arrived home, what did the brothers ask Angelo? (lines 70–71)

_____

5. What was Angelo's favorite part of going to the games? (lines 73–75)

_____

Use reading skills: Compare and contrast.

You **compare** things when you look at how they are the same. You **contrast** them when you look at how they are different. In this article, the brothers compared and contrasted two sports, showing ways they are the same and ways they are different.

Compare and contrast.   In the following paragraphs, Matt and Ricky talk about one way that basketball and baseball are alike.

> "You're too into basketball," Ricky tells his brother. "I'd much rather watch a baseball game. There's more strategy in baseball."
>
> "Are you kidding me?" Matt replies. "Basketball's full of strategy. Who's going to pass? Who's going to take the shot? Basketball is all about strategy."

1. According to the paragraph, what is one way in which basketball and baseball are the same?

    _____

2. What is one way in which basketball and baseball are different?

    _____

Use a graphic organizer.

You can use a graphic organizer like the Venn diagram below to compare and contrast two things. Use the information in the story and what you know from your own experience to compare and contrast basketball and baseball. List things that are alike and different.

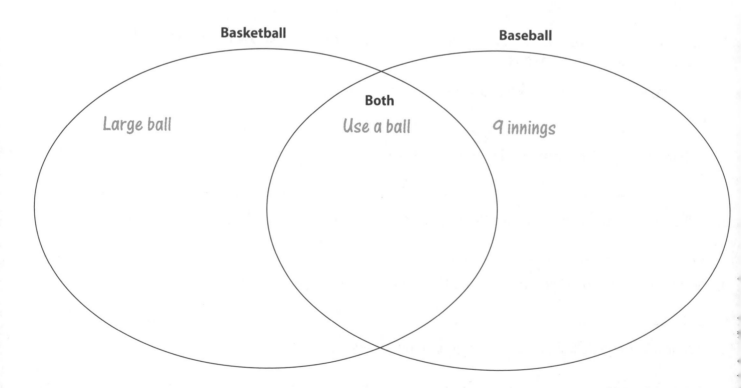

Write About It

Write a recommenation.

The director of your local community center is thinking about starting either a baseball or basketball team. He asked you to make a recommendation. Use the information below and from the article to list the facts about each sport in the chart. Write a recommendation and support your opinion with facts.

Each baseball team should have 16–20 players since not all the players can be at every game. Also, a different player pitches each game so 4–5 pitchers are needed. Each player must have a glove and spikes. There is a special glove for the catcher. The catcher also needs a chest protector, mask, and shin guards. You will need bats, batting helmets, uniforms, and a lot of baseballs. The game must be played on a baseball field with bases and a pitcher's mound. It is hard to play baseball with fewer than nine players on the field.

Basketball teams should have 8–10 players but only five play at one time. Every player needs a uniform consisting of a shirt and shorts and a pair of basketball sneakers. A bag of basketballs is the only equipment you need. The game is played on a court with two baskets and lines for a foul line, half court, and the 3-point arc. Basketball can be played with fewer than five players if both teams have the same number of players on the court.

Prewriting On your own or with a partner, write down ideas you will include in your recommendation. Fill in the Venn diagram with your ideas. Write how the sports are the same and different.

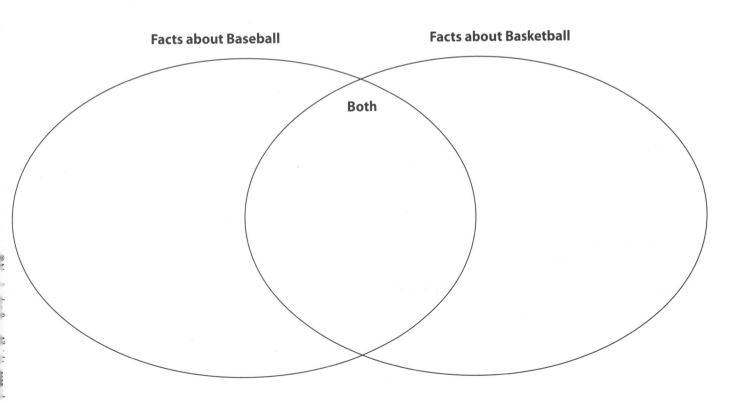

Facts about Baseball   Facts about Basketball

Both

Thinking Beyond Reading   Think about these questions and discuss them with a partner. Add ideas to the graphic organizer as you talk.

- Why did you choose the sport?

- What makes the sport you chose better for the community center?

- What will you need in order to get a team together?

Write a draft.   Write a first draft of your recommendation. Your paragraph might begin with a topic sentence like this one: "I recommend that we start a community _____ team." Use the ideas from your graphic organizer to complete your recommendation.

_____

_____

_____

_____

_____

_____

_____

_____

_____

_____

_____

_____

_____

_____

_____

Revise and create a final draft.   Write your final draft on a separate piece of paper. As you revise, check your draft for these specific points:

- Did you show how the sports are the same and how they are different?

- Did you end with your opinion?

- Did you check spelling and grammar to make sure your writing is clear and correct?

The Way It Was

Learning Objectives

In this lesson you will:

▨ Learn about the Pullman porters of the 1920s.

▨ Learn to make inferences.

▨ Master the key vocabulary used in the article.

▨ Write a summary.

Key Vocabulary

cater *(verb)* to supply people with food and service

dignity *(noun)* state of being worthy of respect

discriminate *(verb)* to treat some people differently than others because they belong to a particular group

economic *(adjective)* of or about money

ensure *(verb)* to make certain

ill *(adjective)* not in good health; sick

luxury *(adjective)* expensive, beautiful, very comfortable

toil *(verb)* to work very hard

transport *(verb)* to carry from one place to another

victory *(noun)* success

Before You Read

As you read the article, you will learn about the problems African American men faced in finding good jobs in the 1920s. Use active reading strategies to understand what these men faced long ago. Ask yourself, "What do I know about problems with finding jobs?" Then, continue asking yourself questions as you read.

Use what you know.

THINK ABOUT IT

1. What problems have you or has someone you know had in finding a good job?

   _____

   _____

   _____

I remember when my father was looking for a good job in an office. They told him he couldn't get hired without a high school diploma. He heard that from a lot of people. So he went back to school.

2. What steps did you or someone else take to solve the problem?

   _____

   _____

   _____

3. What other types of work problems have you heard about?

   _____

   _____

   _____

Ask yourself questions.

THINK ABOUT IT

Read the title of the article and look at the picture on page 77.
1. What questions do you have about them?

   _____

   _____

   _____

Who or what's a Pullman? What's a porter?

2. What other questions do you have about the 1920s?

   _____

   _____

   _____

The Pullman Porters

Read the following article to find out about being a Pullman porter in the 1920s. Jot down on sticky notes questions you have as you read. Look for answers to your questions.

Imagine that it is 1920. You are an African American man with a family to support. You need a job. But well-paying jobs are few and far between.

Times are tough. It is just over fifty years since the end of slavery. Many people **discriminate** against blacks in jobs and education. There are no federal
5 or state laws to ban discrimination in the workplace, as there are today.

What do African American men do for a living in 1920? Some have backbreaking jobs in factories. Others **toil** in the fields. Still others work hard as domestics . These jobs are poorly paid and lack security.

There is a job, though, that is fine for a responsible, hard-working man.
10 That job is being a porter for the Pullman Company. The Pullman Company owns railroad trains. These trains **transport** rich white men and women across the country. Since the trips often take several days, the passengers sleep, eat, and relax on the train. Porters **cater** to the passengers' comfort, helping with the luggage, serving coffee, and making beds.
15 In the 1920s, the Pullman Company needed thousands of porters for their **luxury** trains, known as "hotels on wheels." The company only hired African American men. Although the hours were long, the pay wasn't bad. The work was steady. For a while, many African American men felt lucky to get jobs as Pullman porters.

domestics *(noun)*
house servants

1. Why did some African American men feel the job of porter was OK?

_____

_____

2. Do you think that being a porter was a good job?

_____

_____

Continue reading to find out about the Pullman porters' responsibilities. Look for the answers to the questions asked in the article.

All Aboard?

20   What were the responsibilities of the Pullman porter? When the train pulled into a station, he assisted the men, women, and children in climbing aboard. He carried their luggage up the stairs. But, besides helping people *on* the train, it was also his job to keep some people *off* the train. The porter
25 looked for passengers who were **ill** and stopped them from boarding. The Pullman Company did not want sick passengers spreading disease on the train.

Night and Day

    Each car of the train had two berths , an upper and a lower. These were like bunk beds, one bed on top of the other. At night, the porter made up all
30 the berths in his car. For the upper berth, he pulled down the bed from its place in the ceiling. For the lower berth, he folded down the seats. Then he added blankets, pillows, and sheets to each bed.

    Said one elderly man who rode the train as a child, "I watched the porter make up the beds in the morning and at night. It was tricky. We all woke up
35 and went to bed at different times. But the guy was a pro."

    The porter had other responsibilities as well. During the day, he cleaned the bathroom and handrails, and he polished mirrors. He served food and drinks, lit cigarettes, and sent mail and telegrams. He cared for babies and toddlers. At night, while passengers slept, he brushed passenger's coats and
40 pressed men's jackets and pants. Throughout the day, he followed the Pullman Company's rulebook which had instructions on how to **ensure** passenger safety. He kept order in his car.

    The Pullman porter worked hard, putting in about 400 hours per month. When and how did he sleep? He slept only when his work was done or when
45 the passengers were asleep. He slept in his uniform, sitting up in a chair.

The Good News

    The job was tough, but were there advantages to it? Yes! For one, it was less physically demanding than working on a farm or in a factory. In addition, the Pullman porter got to travel around the country seeing different places and meeting

50 new people. He dressed in a clean uniform instead of the dusty overalls worn by a farmhand. With a steady job, he was respected by people in his community. He was admired by women who saw a Pullman porter as a "good catch."

3. Make a list of the advantages of being a Pullman porter in the 1920s.

_____

_____

Finish reading the article. See if you can answer the questions in the rest of the article. Underline each sentence that tells what the porters union accomplished for its members.

And the Bad News

The job got respect from outsiders, but it felt unfair to the porters
55 themselves. Why? Because much of their pay came from tips from passengers, and some passengers did not tip well. Porters had to buy their own food. And they had to give the company money if a passenger stole a towel. Many porters felt used. After all, their good work was in part responsible for the growth in railroad travel around the country.

60 ### The First Black Union

In 1925, the porters formed the first black labor union. A union would make them better able to meet with the owners of the Pullman Company. It would help them fight for better wages and fewer work hours. The union members elected A. Philip Randolph president of the Brotherhood of Sleeping Car Porters.
65 Under Randolph's leadership, the union won a good contract . After 12 years of bargaining , they got a basic monthly pay hike from $77.50 to $89.50. Tips were extra. They also got a 240-hour work month, down from 400 hours.

As members of the first black union, the men gained even more respect from their friends and neighbors. The contract was a **victory** for the union and
70 for Randolph. As a great-grandson of a Pullman porter said, "Randolph didn't just get better pay for the porters. He brought them **dignity,** too."

After the 1960s, fewer people rode trains. Do you know why? People took cars or planes instead. So the Pullman Company went out of business and porters were not needed. But the Pullman porters and their union had made
75 history. In many ways, they paved the way for the pride and **economic** success of African American men of today.

4. How do you think the Pullman porters felt about their jobs after the contract was signed?

_____

_____

contract (noun)
a legal agreement between two or more people

bargaining (verb)
discussing what will be included in a work contract

After You Read

Build a robust vocabulary.

Writing Sentences   Write a complete sentence to respond to each of the following questions or statements. Use the underlined word in your answer. Use the definitions on page 75 to help you.

1. Tell about a time you achieved a <u>victory</u>.

    _____

2. Describe a time you were too <u>ill</u> to go out.

    _____

3. Would you ever <u>discriminate</u> against someone else?

    _____

4. What is a good way to <u>transport</u> large items to another city?

    _____

5. What is a common <u>economic</u> issue people face?

    _____

Sentence Completions   Complete each sentence using a word from the box.

cater	dignity	discriminate	economic	ensure
ill	luxury	toil	transport	victory

1. The family traveled on a _____ train.

2. The farmer had to _____ for hours in the sun.

3. The union worked to give _____ to the porters.

4. The waitress will _____ to us when she serves lunch.

5. The company will _____ good pay for overtime.

Word Building   The **past tense** of verbs shows actions that happened in the past.

Look at the following words. What is the same about all of them?

touched	missed	picked	washed

Each word has an *-ed* ending. This means the action happened in the past. For example, *touch* becomes *touched*, *miss* becomes *missed*.

Sometimes a short verb changes its spelling before you make it past tense. If the verb has a short vowel, double the last letter before you add -ed. For example, hop becomes hopped, fit becomes fitted. If an action word ends in a consonant and y, then change the y to i before adding -ed. For example, try becomes tried and fry becomes fried.

Write a sentence using the past tense of each verb.

1. pat: _____

2. guess: _____

3. work: _____

4. cry: _____

5. step: _____

TIP: When you read, you may find some verbs you do not know. Think: Did the action happen in the past? Does the word have an -ed ending? Did the word change a y to i before adding -ed?

Writing Activity   Write a short paragraph that correctly uses key vocabulary words to tell about an older person you have known. Use at least four of the words from the list on page 75. Reread the definitions, if necessary.

_____

_____

_____

_____

Think about your reading.

Check your comprehension.   Answer each question. If you don't know the answer, reread the lines in parentheses.

1. What kinds of laws about jobs do we have today that were not in place in the 1920s? (lines 4–5)

_____

2. When did Pullman porters get to sleep on the train? (lines 44–45)

_____

3. Who was A. Philip Randolph? (lines 63–64)

_____

4. What did the Brotherhood of Sleeping Car Porters accomplish? (lines 65–67)

_____

Use reading skills: Make inferences

When you make an **inference,** you use ideas and information that you already have and add other ideas and information. This will help you to figure out something that is not directly stated in the article.

Make inferences.   Read the following paragraphs about what A. Philip Randolph did for the Pullman porters.

> Under Randolph's leadership, the union won a good contract. After 12 years of bargaining, they got a basic monthly pay hike from $77.50 to $89.50. Tips were extra. They also got a 240-hour work month, down from 400 hours.
>
> As members of the first black union, the men gained even more respect from their friends and neighbors. The contract was a victory for the union and for Randolph. As a great-grandson of a Pullman porter said, "Randolph didn't just get better pay for the porters. He brought them dignity, too."

1.   List all the things Randolph got for the porters.

_____

2.   What do you know about how people usually feel about someone who gives them many good things?

_____

3.   Now, put all this information together and make an inference. How did the members of the union probably feel about Randolph?

_____

Use a graphic organizer.

Here is a graphic organizer that helps you put information together to make an inference. Use the information from above to fill in the boxes.

What You Read	What You Know
1. *He got them a contract.* 2. 3.	4.

Make an Inference
5.

Write About It

Write a Summary

A summary is a short piece of writing that gives the most important information from a longer piece of writing. When you write a summary, you write only the main points. You leave out the details. Write a summary of one section of the article you have just read.

Prewriting   Fill out the graphic organizer with the main points of "The Good News" section of the article you have just read. This section tells the advantages of being a Pullman porter, so that is the overall point. Fill in each oval with one advantage, or important point, from that section of the article.

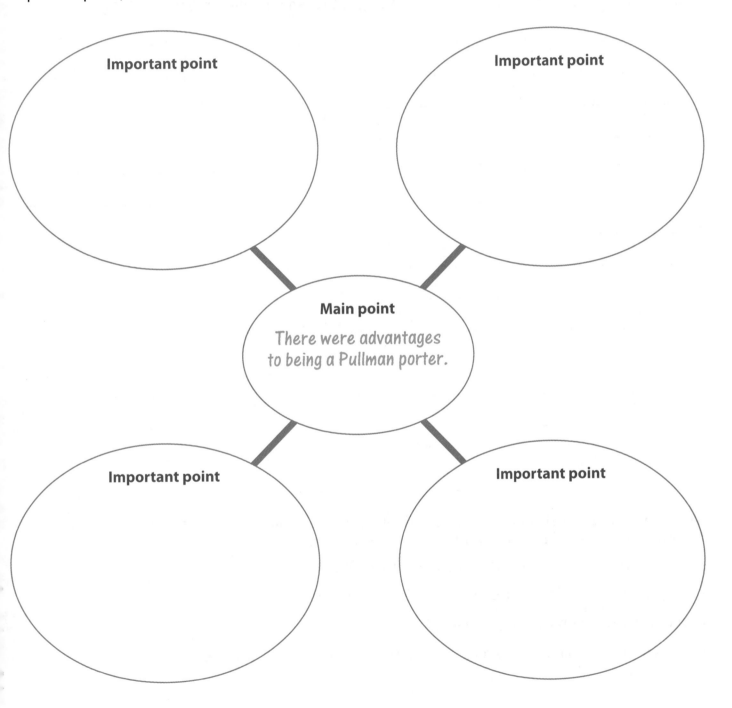

Important point

Important point

Main point

There were advantages
to being a Pullman porter.

Important point

Important point

Thinking Beyond Reading   Think about these questions and discuss them with a partner. Add ideas to the graphic organizer as you talk.

- What other jobs were possible for black men in the 1920s?

- What kinds of things did the Pullman porters do?

- Why were Pullman porters respected?

- Why were Pullman porters admired by women?

Write a draft.   Write a first draft paragraph of your summary. Include only the main points that tell the advantages of being a Pullman porter. Start your summary with a topic sentence, such as, "There were advantages to being a Pullman porter."

_____

_____

_____

_____

_____

_____

_____

_____

_____

_____

_____

_____

_____

_____

Revise and create a final draft.   Write your final draft on a separate piece of paper. As you revise, check your draft for these specific points:

- Did you include a topic sentence that states the overall point?

- Did you write several sentences that give only the main points?

- Did you leave out unnecessary details?

- Did you check spelling and grammar to make sure your writing is clear and correct?

Food Around the World

Learning Objectives

In this lesson you will:

▥ Learn about foods in different countries.

▥ Learn to synthesize information.

▥ Master the key vocabulary used in the article.

▥ Write a paragraph about a personal experience.

Key Vocabulary

ancient *(adjective)* very old

climate *(noun)* the usual weather in a place

consumed *(verb)* eaten

crave *(verb)* to have a strong desire for something

delicacy *(noun)* something good to eat that is expensive or difficult to get

drastically *(adverb)* extremely

ingredients *(noun)* foods that are used to make something

nourishing *(adjective)* making you strong and healthy

substance *(noun)* something that has weight and takes up space; matter

traditional *(adjective)* usual or customary

Before You Read

In this article you will learn about some foods people from different countries eat. Use some active reading strategies to help you understand what you're reading. Ask yourself what you already know about foods from around the world. What do you think you'll learn about?

Use what you know.

THINK ABOUT IT

1. What do you like to eat for dinner?

   _____

   _____

   _____

2. Who do you usually eat dinner with?

   _____

   _____

   _____

I eat a lot of burgers and chicken, but I'm not sure what people in a lot of other countries eat. I'll read to find out.

Make predictions while you read.

THINK ABOUT IT

1. What foods do you eat for dinner? Which of these do you think will be mentioned in the article?

   _____

   _____

   _____

I think the article will talk about what people eat and why they eat it.

2. Do you think the article will discuss why food in other countries is different from American food? Why or why not?

   _____

   _____

   _____

3. What other topics do you think might be included in the article?

   _____

   _____

   _____

What's for Dinner?

Read the article to find out about popular foods in other countries. Use sticky notes to mark the countries and their foods.

Think back to what you had for dinner last night. What did you and your family eat? Chicken with green beans? Steak and potatoes? Burgers and fries? How about meatballs and spaghetti? For families across the United States, these are typical dinners.

5   But have you ever stopped to think what people in other countries eat when their families eat dinner? What foods do families in Russia or Switzerland or China enjoy when they sit down for their main meal of the day?

Many people around the world eat the same meals as you do. But even if the **ingredients** are the same, the food is sometimes prepared differently. The food
10   might be made with spices that are unlike ones we know, making the meal look and taste unusual to most Americans. In some cases, the food eaten in other countries is **drastically** different from the food you are used to.

In all cases, however, the food **consumed** around the world reflects a country's **climate,** economy, history, geography, and culture.

15   **Pass the Dumplings**

What foods or drinks do you **crave** when you're cold? Coffee? Steamed vegetables? What about beets? Beets are bright red vegetables. In Russia, with its cold climate and long winters, people want food that will keep them warm and give them energy. One popular Russian dish is a soup called *borscht*. It's made from beets and
20   other vegetables including carrots, onions, and celery. To bring out the flavor, many people spoon sour cream on top. This hot soup is often the first course of a large meal.

A popular and **traditional** Russian main dish is *pelmeni*. Pelmeni is a meat dumpling, made with beef and pork, onions, and pepper. Wrapped in a thin dough, it's boiled in water or meat broth. Many people say that hunters were the

25 first people to make pelmini many years ago. The hunters wanted a light, but **nourishing,** meal to bring with them on long hunting trips.

If you like hamburgers, you probably like beef. And you may like another Russian dish made with meat and onions cooked in a skillet. It's a Russian favorite called *beef stroganoff*. It's served over rice with sour cream. Said one elderly Russian 30 woman now living in the United States, "My grandmother made this dish when I was a kid. I've tried to make it many times, but it never tastes as good as hers."

And if you ever travel to Russia and you don't want borscht, pelmini, or stroganoff, don't worry. The big cities in Russia have most of the same fast-food restaurants we have here in the United States. But the food you'll get there will be 35 more American than Russian.

1. Do you choose to eat certain dishes when it is very cold or hot outside? Explain.

   _____

   _____

2. What is one traditional Russian dish? Why is it right for Russia's climate?

   _____

   _____

Continue reading the article to learn what foods are eaten in other countries. Underline sentences that tell why a food is right for that place.

Say Cheese

Have you ever felt too cold or too tired to go out to buy groceries? That's one reason *fondue* was first created in Europe. Fondue is a meal popular in Switzerland, a country in northern Europe. Many years ago people started making and eating 40 fondue during cold winters when it was hard to get out to buy fresh food. Families found it easier to make a meal out of the bread and cheese already on their shelves.

You make fondue by heating liquid in a pot and then melting cheese in the hot liquid. The fondue is served at a small table with diners sitting around the pot. They put cubes of bread onto long forks. Then they dip their forks into the pot, 45 covering the bread with melted cheese.

There are other kinds of fondue. If diners want to eat beef, chicken, fish, or fresh vegetables, they can dip the food into hot oil instead of cheese. The hot oil cooks the food. For dessert, some people dip fresh fruit into melted chocolate.

When friends and family gather around a fondue pot, they share more than 50 food. Fondue meals are a good way to bring people together.

Hot Pot

You probably cook your food at the stove, then bring it to the table to eat. But in some countries, people cook at the dinner table. In China, Hong Kong, Thailand, and Korea, people sometimes use a *hot pot* to cook with. A hot pot is 55 a heavy pot filled with soup stock and placed and heated in the center of a table.

Small plates filled with fish, chicken, pork, vegetables, and other food are placed around the hot pot. People sit at the table and use forks or chopsticks to dip their food in the pot. They wait for the food to cook, and when it is done, diners dip the food into various spices and sauces. Sitting together around a table as you cook and eat makes it easy to talk with your friends and family.

3. Why is fondue right for living in Switzerland?

_____

_____

4. How does cooking with a hot pot contribute to family life in some Asian countries?

_____

_____

Finish reading the article to find out more about various foods around the world. Underline sentences that tell about foods you'd like to try.

Weird or Wonderful?

Have you ever seen an iguana on TV or at a pet store? An iguana is a reptile with a large round body, short legs, a long tail, and tiny scales. Some iguanas are green, others brown.

For some people in Costa Rica and other Caribbean countries, eating green iguanas is an **ancient** tradition. When cooked with vegetables and ground corn, iguana meat is filled with flavor. Some people say it tastes like chicken. Maybe that's why some people call iguanas "chicken of the trees."

And speaking of reptiles, did you know that snake is a popular dish in some parts of China? Considered a **delicacy,** snake also tastes like chicken and is generally served fried or in a stew. Snake dishes are supposed to help with circulation and keep you warm on a chilly winter day. Hungry, anyone?

Snake is not the only dish you might think is unusual. In parts of Indonesia, a country in Southeast Asia, deep-fried dragonflies serve as an appetizer . On the warm and sunny island of Bali, children hunt for dragonflies and fry them up as snacks. Kids catch the flying insects by using long poles, with a sticky **substance** at the end. Kids poke the dragonfly and the insect sticks to the tip. Then they pull off the legs and wings of the fly, chop it up, add other ingredients, wrap it in a banana leaf, cook, and eat it.

Asked if he would ever eat this high- protein appetizer, one New Yorker replied, "If I were in Bali, and I was very hungry, I might. But I doubt it."

5. Pick one dish that you think you'd like to eat? Why?

_____

_____

reptile *(noun)*
a cold-blooded animal that crawls across the ground or creeps on short legs, such as a turtle, lizard, or snake

circulation *(noun)*
the movement of blood through the body

appetizer *(noun)*
a small amount of food or drink served at the beginning of a meal

protein *(noun)*
a natural food source found in eggs, milk, fish, and meat

After You Read

Build a robust vocabulary.

Writing Sentences   Write a complete sentence to respond to each of the following statements. Use the underlined word in your answer. Use the definitions on page 85 to help you.

1. Name a <u>traditional</u> American food.

    _____

2. Tell about a time when your life changed <u>drastically</u>.

    _____

3. Tell about the <u>climate</u> in your area.

    _____

4. Name a food you consider a <u>delicacy</u>.

    _____

5. Tell about a food you sometimes <u>crave</u>.

    _____

Sentence Completions   Complete each sentence using a word from the box.

ancient	climate	consumed	crave	delicacy
drastically	ingredients	nourishing	substance	traditional

1. What are the _____ in your favorite soup?

2. Those old books are so _____ they're falling apart.

3. Ken wiped the sticky _____ off his hands with a wet towel.

4. It's important for children to eat a _____ breakfast every morning.

5. The amount of food _____ at the party was amazing!

Word Building   A **root word** is the main part of a word. It contains the basic meaning of the word. For example, in *replacement*, the word *place* is the root word. Look at the following sentence from the article.

> The food might be made with spices that are unlike ones we know, making the meal look and taste unusual to most Americans.

Unlike, unusual, and *Americans* have all been formed from root words. Circle the root in each word. Check your answers with a partner.

Look at the words below. What is the same about all of them?

replace	places	placement	misplace

They all include the root word *place*. Write two sentences. Use one of the words above in each sentence.

1. _____

2. _____

TIP: When you read, you may find some long words that you do not know. Does the word have a root that you do know? Look closely to see if the root word hints at the word's meaning.

Writing Activity   Write a short paragraph that correctly uses key vocabulary words to tell about a meal you remember. Use at least four of the words from the list on page 85. Reread the definitions, if necessary.

_____

_____

_____

_____

_____

Think about your reading.

Check your comprehension.   Answer each question. If you don't know the answer, reread the lines in parentheses.

1. What is the main ingredient in borscht? (lines 18–20)

_____

2. Why was fondue first created? (lines 37–41)

_____

3. Why is snake good for your health? (lines 71–72)

_____

4. How are dragonflies prepared for eating in Bali? (lines 77–78)

_____

_____

_____

Use reading skills: Synthesize information.

When you **synthesize,** you take parts of what you read and put them together to reach a new understanding. For example, if you read about how to plant flowers, feed flowers, and water flowers, you could synthesize that information to explain how to grow flowers.

Synthesize information.   Reread these paragraphs from the article. As you read, put together pieces of information.

> You make fondue by heating liquid in a pot and then melting cheese in the hot liquid. The fondue is served at a small table with diners sitting around the pot. They put cubes of bread onto long forks. Then they dip their forks into the pot, covering the bread with melted cheese.
>
> There are other kinds of fondue. If diners want to eat beef, chicken, fish, or fresh vegetables, they can dip the food into hot oil instead of cheese. The hot oil cooks the food. For dessert, some people dip fresh fruit into melted chocolate.
>
> When friends and family gather around a fondue pot, they share more than food. Fondue meals are a good way to bring people together.

Use what you read to synthesize information about eating fondue.

1. What you read: _People sit around the fondue pot._

2. What you read: _They also talk._

3. What you synthesize: _____

Use a graphic organizer.

You can use a graphic organizer like the one below to help you synthesize information. Fill in the graphic organizer to synthesize information from the second paragraph.

What you read	1. There are other kinds of fondue.
What you read	2.
What you synthesize	3.
What you synthesize	4.

Write About It

Write a paragraph about a personal experience.

Have you ever eaten at a fondue restaurant? A Russian restaurant? A Chinese restaurant? Write a paragraph telling about a visit to a restaurant that serves food that is from another country. Tell about how you felt about the food. Assume that you never tried it before.

Prewriting   Fill in the graphic organizer with your ideas. On your own or with a partner, write down what happened at the restaurant. End the paragraph with your opinion of the restaurant. You may want to add lines to the chart.

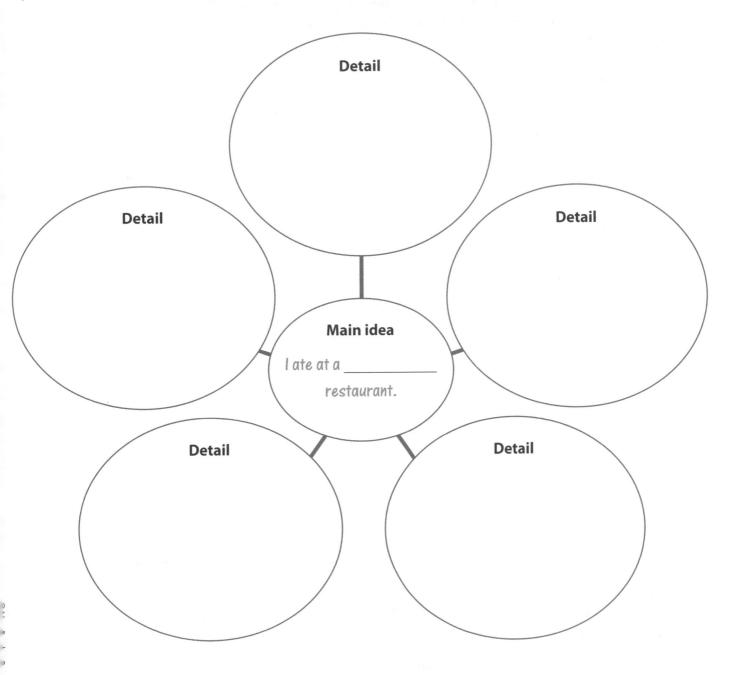

Detail

Detail

Detail

Main idea

I ate at a _____ restaurant.

Detail

Detail

Thinking Beyond Reading   Think about these questions and discuss them with a partner. Add more ideas to the graphic organizer as you talk.

- Which restaurant did you visit?

- What did you eat?

- What was the food like?

- Would you recommend this food to a friend? Why or why not?

Write a draft.   Write a first draft paragraph that tells your story about eating at the restaurant. Your paragraph might begin with this topic sentence: "I had an interesting meal at a Thai restaurant." Use the key ideas you listed in your chart to complete your paragraph. Add as many details as you can.

_____

_____

_____

_____

_____

_____

_____

_____

_____

_____

_____

_____

_____

_____

_____

_____

Revise and create a final draft.   Write your final draft on a separate piece of paper. As you revise, check your draft for these specific points:

- Did you write a topic sentence that sums up the main point of the paragraph?

- Did you include details to support the main idea?

- Did you check spelling and grammar to make sure your writing is clear and correct?

Buying and Selling

Learning Objectives

In this lesson you will:

▓ Read a story about teens who buy and sell stolen goods.

▓ Learn to draw conclusions.

▓ Master the key vocabulary used in the story.

▓ Write a journal entry.

Key Vocabulary

abruptly *(adverb)* very quickly

appraising *(verb)* judging

defensively *(adverb)* in a way to defend your actions

deliberately *(adverb)* on purpose

hesitated *(verb)* waited before doing something

marveled *(verb)* was filled with surprise or amazement

obsession *(noun)* something you think about all the time

outraged *(adjective)* very angry

rationalize *(verb)* to find reasons for doing something

rifling *(verb)* to search through items fast and carelessly

Before You Read

As you begin this story, you might wonder what the deal with the devil is. Keep that question in mind as you read the story. Active readers "talk back" to the writer. They think of questions they want answered as they read.

Ask yourself questions.

1. What do you think the title might mean?

_____

_____

_____

_____

_____

2. Look at the picture on page 97. What questions do you have about it?

_____

_____

_____

_____

_____

Visualize the action in the story.

1. Picture yourself as one of the teens gathered around Sam at the beginning of the story. Does the scene seem real? Tell about groups like this that you know about.

_____

_____

_____

_____

The Devil's Deal

How far are you willing to go to get something you really want? Highlight or mark sentences that give hints about how far Max will go.

"Nice machine." The teenagers clustered around Sam, who had something in his hands. Max went over to see what everyone was so interested in.

"What've you got there?" Max asked, peering at the device Sam was holding.

"It's the new Sajo," Sam said, his thumbs working the device at lightning
5   speed. "It's got streaming video, e-mail, music, movies. You name it."

"Sweet," Max said. "Man, I've seen those. They're about $500. How did you get one? Steal it?"

"Naw," Sam said. "I got it from a friend." TR, who was standing nearby, snickered. So did Rob.

10   "Yeah, he got it from a friend, who got it from another friend. It's good to know friends who can get you whatever you want," TR said. "Right, Sam?"

"Hey," said Sam **defensively,** "If he didn't sell it to me, he'd sell it to someone else. Besides, if some kid is stupid enough to leave out a fine item like this, he gets what he deserves."

15   "What did you pay for it?" Max asked.

"It was a hundred dollars," Sam said.

"No tax," TR smirked.

Max thought about it. So, the Sajo was stolen. Was that so bad? Maybe Sam was right. If some kid was stupid enough not to take care of his stuff, he needed
20   to learn a lesson. Max left the group and shouldered his backpack as he headed to class. That Sajo looked sweet, he thought, really sweet.

1. Why do you think everyone is interested in the Sajo?

_____

_____

2. Why do TR and Rob snicker when Sam says he got the Sajo from a friend?

_____

_____

Max knows the Sajo is probably stolen, but he really wants one. What do you think he will do next? Continue reading to find out the answer.

Max kept thinking about that Sajo. The more he thought about it, the more he wanted it. He could afford $100, but $500 put the Sajo out of reach, which was why he hadn't even thought of getting one. Suddenly he imagined himself with

25 it, listening to music, playing movies. All the rich kids from Highland Heights had one, he knew. They got whatever they wanted, whenever they wanted. As Max thought about it, he got more and more **outraged.** Why should the rich get whatever they wanted, while people like Max watched with envy from the outside? Those rich snobs didn't deserve a Sajo. They wouldn't even appreciate it.

30 It was just another toy to those careless rich kids.

The next day, Max spotted Sam. "Sam," Max said **abruptly.** "That Sajo. I want one. Where do I go?"

Sam looked around quickly, frowning. When he saw they were alone, he shook his head. "Geeze. You think this is some store? Keep your voice down and I'll tell

35 you where to go," Sam said, his own voice low and quiet. "I'll call George and tell him you're coming. Tell him you're a friend of mine."

The whole operation began to seem dirtier and more illegal, but Max was too focused on the Sajo to care. It had become an **obsession.** He wanted it and he didn't care where it came from. The address Sam gave Max was a run-down

40 apartment building on the north side.

Max rang the bell. A guy about 25 with cool gray eyes and a watchful manner opened the door. "George?" Max asked. "I'm Max, Sam's friend."

The man nodded and let Sam in. Inside was a place with electronics stacked in corners—TVs and DVD players, computers, car radios. Max tried to keep his voice

45 level. This guy was more than just a casual thief. This was a business, and a nasty one.

For a second, Max **hesitated.** Did he really want to be a part of this? Then he began to **rationalize.** Rich people were so careless with their stuff, and if they left nice things right out in the open, why shouldn't he benefit? Besides, all they had to do was whine to their parents, who would buy them another one.

50 "I'm looking for a Sajo," Max said. The man nodded shortly, went into the other room, and came back with a Sajo that looked brand new.

"Here you go," the man said, his eyes **appraising** Max.

Max took the Sajo, looking it over. "One hundred dollars?" he asked the man. "That's right," the man said. Max handed over the money and took the Sajo.

3. Do you think Max's reasoning makes sense about buying stolen goods? Why?

_____

_____

4. If you were Max, would you buy the Sajo from George? Why or why not?

_____

_____

Max finally has his Sajo. As you read, underline the sentences that show how he feels about it now.

55　　The Sajo was heaven. Max downloaded movies and tunes and **marveled** at how sharp and clear the picture was, and how true the sound. He **deliberately** didn't think about how he'd scored the Sajo. Max's friend Vinny had seen Max's Sajo and wanted it the same way Max did, but Max was vague when he told Vinny how he'd actually gotten it.

60　　Vinny thought Max had bought the Sajo. Vinny saved the money he made delivering pizza for weeks and finally bought one. "Five hundred, but worth it," Vinny told Max when he showed off his new Sajo. "The thing is awesome."

　　Max had the grace to feel a little ashamed, but he quickly decided that Vinny was just a sucker. Max thought, "Why pay $500 if you don't have to?"

65　　Then Vinny got his brand new Sajo stolen from his locker. Some thieves had gone through the school forcing open lockers and **rifling** through them.

　　So much got taken that the police were called in. They talked to everyone who had something stolen. Three weeks later, the newspaper had a story about an arrest for the thefts. Looking out from the paper was the man Max had bought his

70　　Sajo from. Max rapidly read the story, learning that the man, George Sanderson, had a big business stealing and fencing electronics, computers, and other high-priced items. As Max read on, he got another shock: there were felony arrest warrants out, not just for George Sanderson but for Sam Thurston, who had planned the thefts at North High.

75　　Max's heart pounded as his brain cycled through thoughts of fear and panic—would he be arrested? Then he felt guilt. These were not just Sajos taken from the careless rich, like Sam had said. Max looked down at the stolen Sajo he'd bought. He felt ashamed. He was a criminal. Somewhere deep inside, he'd known that what he did was wrong. That Sajo might have been cheap, but the real cost was in

80　　more than money, and it was more expensive than Max had realized.

fencing (verb)
　　selling stolen goods

felony (noun)
　　a serious crime

arrest warrants (noun)
　　papers that give police the right to arrest people suspected of committing crimes

5. Do you agree with what Max thinks about owning stolen merchandise? Why or why not?

_____

_____

6. What do you think Max will do? Why do you think so?

_____

_____

After You Read

Build a robust vocabulary.

Writing Sentences   Write a complete sentence to respond to each of the following questions or statements. Use the underlined word in your answer. Use the definitions on page 95 to help you.

1. What is something you might have <u>hesitated</u> to do?

   _____

2. How does someone look at you in an <u>appraising</u> way?

   _____

3. Tell about something you might do <u>abruptly</u>.

   _____

4. Tell about something you might be <u>outraged</u> about.

   _____

5. What is something you might <u>rationalize</u> doing.

   _____

Sentence Completions   Complete each sentence using a word from the box.

abruptly	**appraising**	**defensively**	**deliberately**	**hesitated**
marveled	**obsession**	**outraged**	**rationalize**	**rifling**

1. Ana seems to have an _____ about a pair of red shoes she saw in the store.

2. Joe said _____ that he really needed a new car.

3. I _____ did not tell anyone that my birthday was coming soon.

4. All the tourists _____ at the Grand Canyon.

5. The thief was _____ through the drawers in the desk.

Word Building   A **prefix** is a group of letters added at the beginning of a word that changes the word's meaning. For example, you know that the prefix *re-* means "to do again" and the word *rewrite* means "to write again." Here are two other prefixes and their meanings.

Prefix	Meaning
bi-	two
tri-	three

Look at these words. Circle the prefix in each one.

bicycle	**tricycle**	**triangle**	**tricorner**

Write the meaning of each word. Then write a sentence using the word.

1. biplane: _____

   _____

2. bilingual: _____

   _____

3. triathlete: _____

   _____

TIP: Sometimes the prefixes *bi-* and *tri-* are added to a root that is not a whole word. The word *tripod* means "a camera stand that has three legs." A *biped* is "an animal that has two feet."

Writing Activity   Write a short paragraph that correctly uses key vocabulary words to tell how Max felt about buying the stolen Sajo. Use at least four of the words from the list on page 95. Reread the definitions, if necessary.

_____

_____

_____

_____

_____

Think about your reading.

Check your comprehension.   Answer each question. If you don't know the answer, reread the lines in parentheses.

1. What is the price of a Sajo at the store, and the price Sam paid? (lines 6–17)

   _____

2. Where does Max go to get a Sajo? (lines 39–40)

   _____

3. How does Vinny get the money for his Sajo? (lines 60–61)

   _____

4. What part does Sam have in George's operation? (lines 72–74)

   _____

Use reading skills: Draw conclusions.

When you **draw a conclusion,** you think about what you read and add that to information you know from your experiences. Then you draw a conclusion. For example, you might read that a roof is made of packed dirt. Then you read that there is a huge storm. Based on what you know about storms and dirt, you can draw the conclusion that the roof might collapse in the storm.

Draw conclusions.   In the first section of the story, you learn that Sam bought his Sajo from a friend. You know that buying something from a friend instead of a store means that it may be stolen. You can draw the conclusion, based on what you read and what you know, that the Sajo is probably stolen.

Reread this section of the story:

> The next day, Max spotted Sam. "Sam," Max said abruptly. "That Sajo. I want one. Where do I go?"
>
> Sam looked around quickly, frowning. When he saw they were alone, he shook his head. "Geeze. You think this is some store? Keep your voice down and I'll tell you where to go," Sam said, his own voice low and quiet. "I'll call George and tell him you're coming. Tell him you're a friend of mine."

1. What did you learn about the place where Max will buy the Sajo?

   _____

2. What do you know from your experience about that kind of place?

   _____

3. What conclusion can you draw about where Max is buying the Sajo?

   _____

Use a graphic organizer.

You can use a graphic organizer to help you draw conclusions. Two ideas from the story are filled in below. Complete the organizer for each idea. Fill in what you know and the conclusions you draw.

What You Read	What You Know	Conclusions You Draw
George's place is stacked with electronics.	1.	2.
George charges $100 for a Sajo.	3.	4.

Write About It

Write a journal entry.

Imagine that you are thinking about whether to buy, very cheaply, an expensive electronic device you want. You are fairly sure it has been stolen. Write a journal entry that gives the reasons to buy it and not to buy it. Then tell what you will probably do.

Prewriting   You can use the chart below to help you think about the arguments for and against buying the stolen, but inexpensive, electronic device.

Reasons For Buying It	Reasons Against Buying It

What You Will Do

Thinking Beyond Reading   Think about these questions and discuss them with a partner. Add ideas to the graphic organizer as you talk.

• Is it fair that some people have more than others?

• What harm is done by buying stolen goods?

• What are the risks of buying stolen property?

Write a draft.   Write a first draft of your journal entry. Make sure you include the thoughts you have on both sides of the issue. Include the conclusion you reached. You might begin your journal entry with sentences like these: "I am really having trouble making up my mind about buying a stolen electronic device. I can think of reasons for it and against it." Use the organizer you completed to help you write.

_____

_____

_____

_____

_____

_____

_____

_____

_____

_____

_____

_____

_____

_____

_____

Revise and create a final draft.   Write your final draft on a separate piece of paper. As you revise, check your draft for these specific points:

• Did you include reasons both for and against buying the stolen property?

• Did you explain what you decided and why?

• Did you check spelling and grammar to make sure your writing is clear and correct?

Answer Key

Lesson 1 Smart Eating
pp. 5–14

Writing Sentences

Sample answers:

1. I'd <u>encourage</u> someone to lose weight by bringing him on a long walk.
2. An <u>obese</u> person might have diabetes.
3. I <u>avoid</u> fried food.
4. You can live a healthy <u>lifestyle</u> if you don't smoke.
5. A healthy <u>portion</u> of meat should fit in the palm of your hand.

Sentence Completions:

1. joints
2. pressure
3. at risk
4. expert
5. variety

Word Building

Circle *dis-, un-, pre-, dis-, re-*.

Sample answers:

2. Snow in July is very unusual.
3. Let's prearrange where to meet after the concert.
4. My wife and I disagree about buying a new car.
5. Bud likes to replay his favorite videos.

Writing Activity

Answers will vary. Review the vocabulary words and the definitions. Find the words in the article to see how they are used.

Check your comprehension.

Sample answers:

1. An obese person may have diabetes.
2. The family can eat low-fat food at home.
3. A child should get about 60 minutes of activity per day.
4. A good outdoor exercise is jumping rope.

Identify main idea and details.

Sample answers:

1. Detail: An obese person may get heart disease.
2. Detail: An obese person may get diabetes.
3. Detail: The weight presses on the knees, making it painful to walk.

Use a graphic organizer.

Sample answers:

They can dance.

They can play basketball.

Prewriting

Answers will vary, but should include suggestions such as serving smaller portions, serving healthier desserts, and exercising as a family.

Thinking Beyond Reading

The graphic organizer might now include more ways to help a child lose weight.

Write a draft.

Your first draft might begin by summing up the main point of the letter. Include the supporting points you wrote in your graphic organizer.

Revise and create a final draft.

The paragraph should include a topic sentence and details to support the main idea. Sentences should be complete and use correct spelling and punctuation.

Lesson 2 Growing Your Job Possibilities
pp. 15–24

Writing Sentences

Sample answers:

1. Yesterday I smelled my friend's <u>fragrant</u> perfume.
2. An oil and filter change is regular <u>maintenance</u> for most cars.
3. A <u>regional</u> manager must be sure all the stores have the supplies they need.
4. I'm <u>dreading</u> having to do my income taxes.
5. A <u>mature</u> rose bush has many blooms.

Sentence Completions

1. artificial
2. luscious *or* fragrant
3. conferred
4. trowel
5. forged

Word Building

Circle *-ment* in each word.

Sample answers:

1. The children watched the clown with amazement.
2. The band provided excellent entertainment.

3. We all laughed in amusement.

4. Everyone needs encouragement.

5. I hope you get over your disappointment.

Writing Activity

Answers will vary. Review the vocabulary words and the definitions. Find the words in the story to see how they are used.

Check your comprehension.

Sample answers:

1. Rose bushes need lots of sun.

2. He got a job as manager of Cloverdale Nursery.

3. He needed the money.

4. He liked the pay.

5. He wasn't happy with his job.

Identify cause and effect.

Sample answers:

1. He worked indoors.

2. He couldn't meet with customers.

3. He worked on a computer.

4. He worked in artificial light.

5. He analyzed spreadsheets.

6. He conducted meetings.

Use a graphic organizer.

Sample answers:

1. He had a good business sense.

2. He was responsible.

3. He was good with customers.

4. He had a "green thumb."

Prewriting

Sample answers:

1. Planted in fall

2. Planted in shade

3. Didn't water

4. Plant in spring

5. Plant in sun

6. Water well *or* plant in good soil *or* add lime

Thinking Beyond Reading

Answers will vary, but might include that roses need to be planted in spring, six hours of sunlight, rich soil, to be watered, and lime.

Write a draft.

Use the details in your chart to help you write.

Revise and create a final draft.

The paragraph should include a topic sentence with supporting details. Sentences should be complete and use correct spelling and punctuation.

Lesson 3 A New Kind of Family pp. 25–34

Writing Sentences

Sample answers:

1. Paying my car loan is one <u>financial</u> concern of mine.

2. I made a <u>sacrifice</u> to take care of my friend's child while I was on vacation.

3. Health insurance and the economy are <u>issues</u> in today's news.

4. I felt <u>grateful</u> when my boss gave me a raise.

5. A teacher can help her students <u>thrive</u> by giving them extra help after school.

Sentence Completions

1. pampers

2. role

3. neglect

4. assistance

5. violence

Word Building

down/hill, dish/washer, pillow/case, chalk/board

Sample answers:

2. The party will be held in the daytime.

3. When I glanced out the window, I had a daydream.

4. We woke up at daybreak.

Writing Activity

Answers will vary. Review the vocabulary words and the definitions.

Find the words in the article to see how they are used.

Check your comprehension.

Sample answers:

1. More grandparents are raising grandkids.

2. Their own children may be very sick.

3. The parents may be out of work.

4. Some states help pay bills.

Classify information.

Sample answers:

1. The parents are out of a job or there is violence in the home.

2. They are all situations where kids cannot stay with their parents.

Use a graphic organizer.

Sample answers:

Temporary reasons: A parent is in jail. A parent is overseas in the military.

Long-term reasons: There is violence in the home. The parents use drugs.

Prewriting

Answers will vary.

Thinking Beyond Reading

Add new ideas to your graphic organizer.

Write a draft.

Your first draft might begin by summing up the main point of the e-mail, your decision. Include the supporting reasons you wrote in your graphic organizer.

Revise and create a final draft.

The paragraph should include a topic sentence and details to support the main idea. Sentences should be complete and use correct spelling and punctuation.

Lesson 4 Friends and Neighbors
pp. 35–44

Writing Sentences

Sample answers:

1. You could <u>meticulously</u> keep a budget by tracking everything you spend.

2. In our family, three <u>generations</u> are alive.

3. After a storm, boxes in my basement were <u>permeated</u> with water.

4. You can ignore someone having a <u>tantrum</u>.

5. Winter is the season <u>preceding</u> spring.

Sentence Completions

1. abandoned

2. torrent

3. receded

4. frantically

5. horizontally

Word Building

Circle -*d* or -*ed*. Underline *flipped*.

Sample answers:

1. jumped: She jumped over the log.

2. cleaned: I cleaned the kitchen sink.

3. hiked: We hiked up the mountain.

4. flipped: Jo flipped over each card as she played the game.

5. stapled: I stapled the receipts together.

6. washed: Tim washed the car on Saturday.

Writing Activity

Answers will vary. Review the vocabulary words and the definitions. Find the words in the story to see how they are used.

Check your comprehension.

Sample answers:

1. Every evening, Jesse and his father sweep the sidewalk, shut the store, roll down the metal cover and padlock it.

2. The sandbags are to help keep the water from going over the banks of the river.

3. Jesse and his father rush to the store to see what they can do to save it.

4. People come to help Jesse and his father because they think the store is important to the community and because they appreciate all the things Jesse's family has done for them.

Identify cause and effect.

Sample answers:

1. cause

2. effect

3. He feels guilty. He wants to repay Jesse's father.

Use a graphic organizer.

Sample answers:

1. The water floods over the river banks.

2. Customers of the store come to help clean it up.

Prewriting

Answers will vary but may include: a flood swamps the store; customers who feel the store is important to the community come to clean it up; Jesse decides to stay at the store.

Thinking Beyond Reading

Answers might include: feeling that they would also feel stifled if they were in Jesse's shoes; understanding that the store is important because it helps create the community; understanding that Jesse now appreciates the importance of the store to the town and to himself, and is happy being there now.

Write a draft.

Use the important events in your chart to help you write.

Revise and create a final draft.

The paragraph should include the important events that happened, in the correct order. Sentences should be complete and use correct spelling and punctuation.

Lesson 5 Read All About It
pp. 45–54

Writing Sentences

Sample answers:

1. I saw a man being <u>ridiculed</u> at a party.

2. I was <u>embarrassed</u> when I forgot my doctor's appointment.

3. You feel sore when you're <u>bruised</u>.

4. He was <u>gifted</u> in sports.

5. I had to use a <u>manual</u> when I set up my computer.

Sentence Completions

1. humiliation

2. emotionally

3. agency

4. submit

5. invested

Word Building

Circle -*s* or -*es* in each word.

2. sign<u>s</u>

3. letter<u>s</u>

4. coache<u>s</u>

5. agencie<u>s</u>

Sample answers:

6. John was one of the coaches for his son's Little League team.

7. John never learned that the letters had sounds.

Writing Activity

Answers will vary. Review the vocabulary words and the definitions. Find the words in the article to see how they are used.

Check your comprehension.

Sample answers:

1. He had trouble reading manuals, letters, or street signs.

2. He said, "I can't read."

3. He kept silent because he thought it was his fault.

4. His father filled out the job application.

Identify time order words.

1. <u>Towards the end of junior college</u>

2. <u>Then</u>

3. <u>after graduation</u>

4. <u>Years later</u>

5. <u>Today</u>

Use a graphic organizer.

Sample answers:

2. First she found a program that provides tutoring for adults.

3. Then she called them.

4. Then she told the tutor, "I can't read."

5. Finally, the tutor helped her learn to read.

Prewriting

Sample answers:

1. Wash your face and hands.

2. Get dressed.

3. Eat breakfast.

4. Brush your teeth and hair.

5. Gather books, papers, and pencils and put in your backpack.

Thinking Beyond Reading

Answers will vary but might include more things to do to get ready for school.

Write a draft.

Your first draft might begin by summing up the main point of the paragraph. Include the supporting points you wrote in your graphic organizer. Write the points in the order that you numbered them.

Revise and create a final draft.

The paragraph should include a topic sentence and details to support the main idea. Sentences should be complete and use correct spelling and punctuation.

Lesson 6 Hard Work Pays Off
pp. 55–64

Writing Sentences

Sample answers:

1. I saw <u>diversity</u> when a group of people gathered for the Memorial Day parade.

2. My great grandfather went through the <u>immigration</u> process.

3. When someone is <u>evicted</u>, he or she has to find somewhere else to live.

4. I showed <u>persistence</u> when I wanted to lose weight.

5. One of the <u>obstacles</u> I need to overcome is not graduating from high school.

Sentence Completions

1. fluent

2. objectives

3. achievers

4. mission

5. violence

Word Building

Circle *elect, turn, evict, fund, strong.*

Sample answers:

2. turned

3. eviction

4. refund

5. strongest

Writing Activity

Answers will vary. Review the vocabulary words and the definitions. Find the words in the article to see how they are used.

Check your comprehension.

Sample answers:

1. Florida

2. One responsibility is to vote on bills.

3. She came from Cuba.

4. She has supported funding for breast cancer.

5. She has tried to get money to clean up the Miami River.

Make judgments.

Sample answers:

1. women's rights

2. because violence against women is a women's rights issue

3. yes

Use a graphic organizer.

Sample answers:

1. A Congresswoman who supports programs to fight violence against women shows her commitment to women's rights.

2. The Congresswoman does support women's rights.

3. Ros-Lehtinen is Hispanic.

4. She wants other Hispanics to be successful.

Prewriting

Sample activities:

What the editorial says: the plant will bring in new jobs; the air and water can be cleaned up later; people with lung disease can go to a doctor.

What I know: It takes a very long time and lots of money to clean air and water once it is polluted; people with lung disease often don't get well again, even if they go to a doctor.

My judgment: the cement plant should not be opened.

Thinking Beyond Reading

Answers will vary but might include: Workers are needed to run the plant; other businesses support the workers' needs; polluted air and water can't always be cleaned up.

Write a draft.

Use the details in your chart to help you write.

Revise and create a final draft.

The final draft should state your judgment about whether the cement plant should be built and the reasons you think so. Sentences should be complete and use correct spelling and punctuation.

Lesson 7 Everyone's a Winner
pp. 65–74

Writing Sentences

Sample answers:

1. I had to <u>settle</u> an argument between my younger brothers.

2. I'm <u>enthusiastic</u> about soccer.

3. Getting a good education is a <u>strategy</u> for having a successful life.

4. Yes, I think basketball is more <u>intense</u> than golf.

5. I am <u>determined</u> to buy a new car.

Sentence Completion

1. avid

2. elated

3. self-portrait

4. dully

5. draped

Word Building

line/up

Sample answers:

1. The child was very underweight.

2. The hamburger was undercooked.

Writing Activity

Answers will vary. Review the vocabulary words and the definitions. Find the words in the story to see how they are used.

Check your comprehension.

Sample answers:

1. Ricky is wearing a baseball jersey and cap.

2. The brothers first took Angelo to a basketball game.

3. Then they took him to a baseball game.

4. They asked him which sport is more exciting.

5. Angelo's favorite part was being with his uncles.

Compare and contrast.

Sample answers:

1. Basketball and baseball are both games of strategy.

2. A basketball team has five players. A baseball team has nine players.

Use a graphic organizer.

Sample answers:

Basketball: timed, 5 players

Baseball: small ball; 9 players

Both: coach, teams

Prewriting

Answers will vary but may include:

Baseball—16–20 players; 4–5 pitchers; glove and spikes for each; 1 catcher's mitt; 1 chest protector, mask, shin guards; bats; helmets; baseballs; field.

Basketball—8–10 players; sneakers; basketballs; court.

Both—uniforms, balls.

Thinking Beyond Reading

Add new ideas to your graphic organizer.

Write a draft.

Your first draft might begin by summing up the recommendation. Include the supporting points you wrote in your graphic organizer.

Revise and create a final draft.

The paragraph should include a topic sentence and details to support the main idea. Sentences should be complete and use correct spelling and punctuation.

Lesson 8 The Way It Was
pp. 75–84

Writing Sentences

Sample answers:

1. My softball team achieved a <u>victory</u> at the district playoffs.

2. Last winter I had the flu and was too <u>ill</u> to go out for three days.

3. My friends and I try not to <u>discriminate</u> against anyone.

4. We use my uncle's truck to <u>transport</u> large items.

5. A common <u>economic</u> issue today is the high price of gasoline.

Sentence Completions

1. luxury

2. toil

3. dignity

4. cater

5. ensure

Word Building

Sample answers:

1. That little girl patted the cat's head.

2. Emil guessed the teacher's age.

3. My friend worked at the bus stataion.

4. My daughter cried when she fell down the stairs.

5. He stepped out of the way of the car.

Writing Activity

Answers will vary. Review the vocabulary words and the definitions. Find the words in the article to see how they are used.

Check your comprehension.

Sample answers:

1. Today we have federal and state laws that ban discrimination in the workplace.

2. They slept on the train when their work was done and when passengers were sleeping.

3. A. Philip Randolph was president of the Brotherhood of Sleeping Car Porters.

4. It won a contract that reduced the number of hours and increased the pay of the Pullman porters.

Make inferences.

Sample answers:

1. He got a contract, more pay, better hours, and dignity for the porters.

2. They usually feel grateful to the person and give him great respect.

3. They probably admired him and considered him a hero.

Use a graphic organizer.

Sample answers:

2. He got them more pay.

3. He got them better hours *or* dignity.

4. People are grateful and respect someone who does this.

5. A. Philip Randolph was a hero to the Pullman porters.

Prewriting

Answers will vary but may include: the work was easier than other jobs; porters got to see different places and meet new people; they wore clean uniforms; they were respected in the community; they were considered good catches.

Thinking Beyond Reading

The graphic organizer might now include: other jobs included very hard work under difficult conditions; the work of Pullman porters was not backbreaking; Pullman porters wore neat uniforms and had responsibilities on the train; they had good, steady jobs; they made more money.

Write a draft.

Use the details in your chart to help you write.

Revise and create a final draft.

The final paragraph should include a topic sentence and only the main points given in the "The Good News" section of the article. Sentences should be complete and use correct spelling and punctuation.

Lesson 9 Food Around the World
pp. 85–94

Writing Sentences

Sample answers:

1. Apple pie is a <u>traditional</u> American food.

2. My life changed <u>drastically</u> when my daughter was born.

3. Our <u>climate</u> is hot and humid.

4. I think caviar is a <u>delicacy</u>.

5. Sometimes I <u>crave</u> chocolate.

Sentence Completions

1. ingredients

2. ancient

3. substance

4. nourishing

5. consumed

Word Building

Circle *like, usual, America.*

Sample answers:

1. Sarah had to take a placement test before she started school.

2. I lost my watch and now I have to replace it.

Writing Activity

Answers will vary. Review the vocabulary words and the definitions. Find the words in the article to see how they are used.

Check your comprehension.

Sample answers:

1. The main ingredient in borscht is beets.

2. Fondue was first created because families didn't want to go out in the cold to get fresh food.

3. It is said to keep you warm and help your circulation.

4. Dragonflies are prepared by pulling off the legs and wings of the fly, chopping it up, adding other ingredients, wrapping it in banana leaf, and then cooking it.

Synthesize information.

Sample answers:

3. What you synthesize: Eating fondue together brings friends and family together.

Use a graphic organizer.

Sample answers:

2. Some diners want to eat beef, chicken, fish, or fresh vegetables

3. They can dip the food into hot oil or cheese.

4. Different foods can be dipped into different liquids.

Prewriting

Answers will vary.

Thinking Beyond Reading

Answers will vary, but might now include more details about the experience such as how you felt about the food.

Write a draft.

Your first draft might begin by summing up the main point of the paragraph. Include the supporting points you wrote in your graphic organizer.

Revise and create a final draft.

The paragraph should include a topic sentence and details to support the main idea. Sentences should be complete and use correct spelling and punctuation.

Lesson 10 Buying and Selling
pp. 95–104

Writing Sentences

Sample answers:

1. I've <u>hesitated</u> to buy a new car.

2. Someone who looks at you in an <u>appraising</u> way is judging you.

3. I might <u>abruptly</u> change my mind about something.

4. I would be <u>outraged</u> if I saw anyone hurting an animal.

5. I might <u>rationalize</u> eating dessert.

Sentence Completions

1. obsession

2. defensively, abruptly

3. deliberately

4. marveled

5. rifling

Word Building

Circle *bi-* or *tri-* in each word.

1. a plane with two (sets of) wings; I saw a biplane at the air show.

2. speaking two languages; I'm glad that I'm bilingual in Spanish and English.

3. an athlete in three sports; My cousin is training to be a triathlete.

Writing Activity

Answers will vary. Review the vocabulary words and the definitions. Find the words in the story to see how they are used.

Check your comprehension.

Sample answers:

1. A Sajo is $500 in the store, and Sam paid $100.

2. Max goes to George's apartment on the north side.

3. Vinny gets the money for his Sajo by working at the pizza store.

4. Sam planned the thefts from the school lockers.

Draw conclusions.

Sample answers:

1. The place Max will buy the Sajo is not a store.

2. I know that sometimes people sell things from their homes that are stolen.

3. I can draw the conclusion that Max is buying the Sajo from a place that probably sells stolen goods.

Use a graphic organizer.

Sample answers:

1. Someone's house doesn't have all this stuff.

2. George is running a business in stolen goods.

3. This is too cheap.

4. It must be stolen.

Prewriting

Answers will vary but the reasons for buying the stolen electronics might be that they are too expensive to start with; that they are stolen from rich kids who don't appreciate them; that the price is cheaper. Reasons against might be: stealing and buying stolen goods is wrong; buying stolen goods encourages thieves; and buying stolen goods hurts people whose things are stolen. The decision you make might be to not buy stolen goods.

Thinking Beyond Reading

The graphic organizer might now include more details such as these: unfairness doesn't justify theft; theft harms people who have things stolen and harms companies that make things that are stolen; the risks of buying stolen property include going to jail.

Write a draft.

Use the details in your chart to help you write.

Revise and create a final draft.

The final draft should tell both sides of the issue and tell clearly why the writer made the choice he or she did. Sentences should be complete and use correct spelling and punctuation.